Marriage Minded

10 Ways to Know
If You've Found the One

Nick and Chelsea Hurst

 ZONDERVAN
BOOKS

ZONDERVAN BOOKS

Marriage Minded
Copyright © 2023 by Nicholas Hurst and Chelsea Crockett Hurst

Requests for information should be addressed to:
Zondervan, *3900 Sparks Dr. SE, Grand Rapids, Michigan 49546*

Zondervan titles may be purchased in bulk for educational, business, fundraising, or sales promotional use. For information, please email SpecialMarkets@Zondervan.com.

ISBN 978-0-310-36498-6 (audio)

Library of Congress Cataloging-in-Publication Data

Names: Hurst, Nicholas, 1997– author. | Hurst, Chelsea, 1998– author.
Title: Marriage minded : ten ways to know you've found the one / Nick and Chelsea Hurst.
Description: Grand Rapids : Zondervan, 2023. | Summary: "More than 2.4 million people on YouTube watched Nick and Chelsea Hurst journey through dating, engagement, and marriage. In Marriage Minded, the refreshingly honest young couple walk you through the guidance they received, lessons they learned, and questions they asked themselves and others as they navigated the biggest decision of their lives"—Provided by publisher.
Identifiers: LCCN 2022032462 (print) | LCCN 2022032463 (ebook) | ISBN 9780310364962 (hardcover) | ISBN 9780310364979 (ebook)
Subjects: LCSH: Dating (Social customs)—Religious aspects—Christianity. | Courtship—Religious aspects—Christianity. | Mate selection—Religious aspects—Christianity. | Man-woman relationships—Religious aspects—Christianity. | BISAC: RELIGION / Christian Living / Spiritual Growth | FAMILY & RELATIONSHIPS / Marriage & Long-Term Relationships
Classification: LCC BT706 H87 2023 (print) | LCC BT706 (ebook) | DDC 261.8/35—dc23/eng /20221026
LC record available at https://lccn.loc.gov/2022032462
LC ebook record available at https://lccn.loc.gov/2022032463

Published in association with The Bindery Agency, www.TheBinderyAgency.com.

Cover photo: © *Brooke Womack Photography*
Interior design: Sara Colley

Printed in the United States of America

22 23 24 25 26 27 28 29 30   /LSC/   12 11 10 9 8 7 6 5 4 3 2 1

*To every reader of this book who is
searching for the right relationship,
not just the relationship for right now*

CONTENTS

FOREWORD

Being from the Pacific Northwest usually means a few things. One, I (Jeff) have an obvious love for single-origin third-wave coffee (who doesn't?). Two, I don't own an umbrella (that's only for tourists). And three, I grew up with a strange vantage point of marriage and family.

See, Seattle and Portland (where I grew up and where I went to college) tend to have more dogs than children. Marriage is mostly looked down on, and if you do see it, it's rarely healthy or flourishing. The air we breathe in the Northwest is made up of individualism, career obsession, and an overall repulsion to anything that limits us. And marriage sometimes feels limiting, even though Alyssa and I would argue that it's the ultimate freedom.

Take skydiving, for example. You could argue that to be the "most free," you wouldn't want to wear any parachute or restraints. But we know that's dumb. Experiencing the *true freedom* of skydiving (the joy, exhilaration, etc.) actually comes down to knowing you are doing it with the restraints. Living within a design or the confines of something can very much allow for *more* freedom, not less. And in reading Nick and Chelsea's *Marriage Minded*, we felt that exact same wisdom from them.

So many young couples these days are stumbling into marriage with an ideal or set of principles that is a Disney–Tinder–social media cocktail of values, and pain ensues pretty quickly.

Why isn't this marriage satisfying me like I thought it would?

Why is this so painful?

Why is the person I thought I loved now the cause of bitterness and contempt in my heart?

These are questions most young couples are feeling in their hearts, but they don't know how to ask them.

The good news is that you aren't alone. Our culture is designed to set us up with a view of marriage that isn't helpful. I still remember feeling this pain point in year two for Alyssa and me because one thing most folks didn't set us up for was the fact that marriage is a collision of the worst and best parts of yourself with the exact same things in another.

And until we wrestle with the fact that *this is by design*, we won't understand how to flourish in a marriage.

Marriage, unlike what Disney movies have led you to believe, is less about personal fulfillment and more about personal transformation! Marriage is designed by God to be one of the single most powerful tools for taking the parts of you that need some work or that you don't love—your weaknesses, frailties, and more—and softly, gently healing and reworking those things into parts of you that bring blessing and goodness to others, not hurt.

God and marriage are a little bit like going to the dentist. If you're anything like us, almost every time we go to the dentist, he discovers something much worse than what we went in for. We go in to get our teeth clean, and we leave with an appointment for a root canal. But that means that once the dentist lays eyes on our teeth, it's his duty to bring us to full health. And sometimes marriage feels a bit like this. We know we have some blind spots and weaknesses, but once we look under the hood and get into a marriage that reveals them all under a spotlight, we realize just how many more blind spots and weaknesses we have.

The good news is that amid all that, we also realize that *we are more deeply loved than we could ever imagine!* And that's the paradox and blessing of a marriage on fire. The more we lean into the difficulty—if we're equipped by God with the good news of the gospel and the Spirit's help—we will also find love and intimacy like we've never known.

Jefferson and Alyssa Bethke

PREFACE

Sitting in Your Questions with You

Nick and Chelsea

Chelsea

It was the fall of 2003 in small-town Troy, Illinois. I packed up my kindergarten lunch box in our family kitchen with my mom and got ready to head to school. I always loved these mornings because I looked forward to school. Maybe it was all the fun activities we did, like the science experiments I got to be a part of in the morning. Or maybe (honestly) I was looking forward to seeing my kindergarten crush, Connor. Connor had dark brown hair, a soft dimple on the left side of his face, and an eagerness to spend time with me every day. Even though the other boys would make fun of him for playing with me, I felt important and special because he always chose to hang out with me instead of the other kids in our class. Every day, we played my favorite game (house), acting out the roles of mom and dad. We didn't involve any of our classmates because we enjoyed being our own little family all by ourselves. Every day, we cleaned up

our Fisher Price kitchen, made our make-believe dinner, and vacu-
umed our little corner rug. At the end of this afternoon routine, we
kissed each other on the cheek before we went to our make-believe
"jobs." Looking back on this time a couple of decades later, I see a
desire from childhood that never went away. I wanted to be loved and
adored by someone and give love to them too. My pretend kindergarten boyfriend and I both wanted to carry on what we saw as an
example in our parents' marriages. We looked up to our parents in
many ways because they taught us what love looks like. They showed
us how to communicate, give affection and affirmation, and treat
each other with respect.

Growing up in a small town, I quickly got to know the few boys
who were a part of my school and community. Most of them were
from farming families and liked to make fun of us girls as a form of
flirting. I never understood why they considered that flirting, but
"boys will be boys," right? In middle school, my girlfriends and I
owned the pink Razr smartphones or the phones that slid to text.
We felt so cool, because in our little world we were. We were enam-
ored with Sillybandz, electric scooters, and weekends spent at the
skating rink. At sleepovers with my girlfriends, we'd get on Facebook
Messenger and send a bunch of messages to boys from nearby towns,
using "pre–emoji days" faces. They looked like this, if you recall:

:D

;P

And, boy, were you flirting if you threw in a face like that!

Today it seems so hard to really get to know another person with
the barriers that social media and countless online distractions put
in our lives. We've progressed so quickly from pink Razr phones to
advanced computers in our pockets. We were created for rich and
deep community, and the overstimulation of constant online connection with everyone can cause issues in relationships if we aren't
careful.

Very often in my dating journey, I asked myself some serious questions. I grew tired of dating for fun and wanted my next relationship to be with the man I would marry. In my previous relationships I found myself going back and forth in my head with a lot of questions:

- *How do I know if this is the person God has for me?*
- *We come from really different backgrounds. Can we still make it work?*
- *How do we build a strong relationship in God that will last even when we struggle?*
- *What does it take to stay committed?*
- *I'm bringing some "baggage" into this relationship—how do I talk with my boyfriend about it and keep it from damaging our relationship?*
- *My boyfriend seems to be struggling to commit. Is it me? Or him? Or the relationship?*
- *I need clarity about what is healthy and what isn't healthy. Good relationship for right now? Or the right relationship for good?*

I was so frustrated with feeling like I lived in the same cycle: getting to know a new guy, trusting and opening up to him, and then realizing through questions like these (and by dating him far too long) that he was not meant to be my husband. I wish I'd had someone to walk me through what to consider or how to know I'd found my future husband—and then where to go next. At first, these questions used to stump me and keep me from moving forward, but in the right relationship, they helped me and Nick ask the important questions and focus on each other and our direction moving forward.

More than anything else, before I got married I recall desiring that the relationships I was in would be "the one," and I wanted each next relationship to be the last time I had to think about opening up my heart again, getting to know someone, and taking the risk of trusting another person deeply. Before I met Nick, I dated a man who was a Christian—he was strong and kindhearted too. I thought we had potential for marriage moving forward, but a few months into dating, God woke me up to some things that were lacking in me and in the relationship. A lot of them had to do with not being of the same mind spiritually, and I found I was treating him as if he would fulfill me. It is very possible to date a Christian but to have differing convictions. I still had some growing I needed to do, and so did he. Thankfully, we broke up and both saw goodness in that as time went on and we grew apart. There was someone who was a better fit for each of us, and as I look back I'm so glad we didn't try to force the relationship to work.

It was scary sometimes, thinking about putting so much time and effort into something that might not work out, and most times it just didn't seem worth it if there was the chance it would end. If this has been your pattern in the past, you are not alone! I wish I'd had someone to remind me of what matters and of what I should have been putting my focus on in my dating relationships.

After sitting with all my questions, I had a moment with God. I was serious about not making a move into a new relationship if it wasn't from him. As I sat in the middle of my bed, I stared at the ceiling and wrote my final words into the journal I had used to write about all my guy problems. "There has to be more to relationships than what I have experienced in the past. There must be! Lord, I want to be in the right relationship with my future husband, or I don't want a relationship at all." I closed my journal I had written in for the past year and slid it under my bed.

I didn't know all the journal entries I had written through the years would point to the faithfulness of God, but every time I read them, I am brought to tears. The Lord cares more than you do about your future and who you spend it with. You know all the countless nights you sat awake, wondering how your life would play out? Who would your future friends be? Would you be living in a different city? Would you have kids one day? What job would you have? These questions kept me up through the night: *What is God going to make of my future?* I now know it is amazing that I even get to have a relationship with my heavenly Father and that we get to play a part in what he is doing here on earth!

Nick and I have spent years thinking, praying, writing, and intentionally working toward writing this book that we hope can meet you where you're at. But first of all, we truly believe all these suggestions, stories, Bible verses, and words of encouragement will mean nothing without first knowing Jesus. You cannot "self-help" yourself into a lifelong, committed marriage without the power of Jesus and his grace. We also realize any piece of writing founded on what we've learned by walking with Christ keeps the audience of this book smaller. That is perfectly okay with us, and we want our intentions to be clear from the start! Anything that we have learned in this process is all because Jesus is alive and wants to speak through his Word and through his people, and he cares for you and how you spend your life and eternity.

> **You cannot "self-help" yourself into a lifelong, committed marriage without the power of Jesus and his grace.**

GOSPEL CALL

I'd love to share with you how Jesus absolutely changed my life. I remember as a ten-year-old asking my parents about salvation and telling them I wanted to give my life to Jesus. I believe my decision was genuine, but I didn't begin following Jesus until high school. I had believed that God was there for me, but I didn't walk with him daily until a Discipleship Now event. The preacher shared about sin and life apart from Christ, and I immediately felt a conviction in my heart, knowing he was talking to me. What he was sharing resonated deeply. At that moment I asked the Lord to forgive me of my sins and to start walking with me daily in relationship.

If you don't have a relationship with Jesus, I would love to share with you the greatest story ever told. This is the gospel in the Word of God (*gospel* means "good news").

> For God so loved the world that he gave his one and only Son, that whoever believes in him shall not perish but have eternal life. (John 3:16)

> If you declare with your mouth, "Jesus is Lord," and believe in your heart that God raised him from the dead, you will be saved. For it is with your heart that you believe and are justified, and it is with your mouth that you profess your faith and are saved. As Scripture says, "Anyone who believes in him will never be put to shame." For there is no difference between Jew and Gentile—the same Lord is Lord of all and richly bless-es all who call on him, for, "Everyone who calls on the name of the Lord will be saved." (Romans 10:9–13)

> It is by grace you have been saved, through faith—and this is not from yourselves, it is the gift of God, not by works, so that no one can boast. (Ephesians 2:8–9)

Every time I read these verses, I am amazed at the grace of God for you and me! What a beautiful gift we have. What a wonderful Savior and mighty Counselor. If you would like to begin a relationship with Jesus and commit your life and future to him, say this prayer. Speak it from your heart if you believe God is calling you into a relationship with him.

Lord Jesus, thank you for saving me. I believe you died on the cross as a sacrifice for me and others, for the sins of the world (my sins included). I am so undeserving of your love, but I thank you for lavishing your love on me through your Son. I admit that I am a sinner and I no longer want to walk this life alone.

If you said that prayer, we are jumping up and down for you! Seriously, if you entered into a relationship with Jesus because of this chapter, message us and we will send you a video back! We encourage you to get plugged into a local church where you can grow with other believers. If you need help with this process, we would love to be there for you.

Reflecting

I'm not sure how you met your boyfriend or girlfriend, and maybe recalling the story brings all sorts of emotions to the surface. I love talking about when Nick and I met. We met on Twitter, and I never expected in a million years for that to be the case, but a few weeks later we knew to take the relationship from phone to in person. It was just the next step for us with the peace that God had given us about the friendship we had formed. I look back and see the faithfulness of Jesus in taking two broken people and allowing them to build a life together. You know your story better than anyone else, but there are a few things (we hope this book can provide those things!) to think about before moving into marriage. I'm so grateful for the consistent couples who shaped my views and boundaries as a woman desiring marriage, as they set the tone for the marriage I have with Nick.

Nick and I have a son named Hudson, and he is the biggest blessing of our lives! I remember thinking early on in dating that I could see Nick becoming a great father because he had the heart of a father already for his friends and family. Even if you never have children, having a father's heart (like the Lord's heart for us) is a blessing to others, and it is a quality that is hard to come by. Someone willing to sit down and offer up wisdom from good and bad experiences, willing to lay down their life for another, one who doesn't judge first but rather loves—that is rare!

I was a big journaler in my youth. I love writing letters, and I believe I have an old soul. I am moved by the way a letter can carry emotion and memories in a unique way. A video on our YouTube channel shares the letters I wrote to my future husband from as young as twelve or thirteen years old. Yes, the letters were a little "cringey" to read, as I had no idea what I was talking about, and you would assume based on my writing that I watched way too many cheesy romance movies. But I love going back and reading them. I can see the kindness of God woven through the desires placed on paper and how he shifted them into godly desires.

Idea to try: I am so glad that as a teenager I decided to write prayers, along with letters, to my future spouse. It was such a fun thing to record my journey and to write to Nick years before meeting him. It's never too late to start doing this, even if you're already engaged. In these letters and prayers, share the date and what you've been praying for, as well as your heart and your struggles at the time. I have letters from when I was thirteen years old, as well as from a month before I got married to Nick. The letters I wrote from a hurting heart when I had gone through a breakup are kind of funny looking back. I had a lot to learn through those years, and it is amazing to see God's hand through it all. Through letter writing and journaling, you'll find that our God is in the business of answering prayers, and you'll see his faithfulness throughout your life and the life of your future spouse.

As you reflect on the type of person you desire to marry, and the person you are as well, you'll realize that while there are flaws within you both, a steady commitment to growth is necessary. God will show you when the time is right to move forward as you pursue him above all. The person we choose to be with will never be our savior and never should be! There are needs that we have as humans that only the Lord can meet. Your future spouse cannot meet your every need. But they will play a key role in the way you live out your purpose on this earth. With intentionality and the help of the Holy Spirit, you can get your heart and mind in the right place, as well as be honest with yourself about whether you are ready for the next step in your relationship.

Also, I feel now is a great place to mention that as you go through this book and have intentional conversations, if there are signs of not wanting to pursue this relationship anymore, and God is showing you that—you can do hard things! It is important that you choose to be with someone who is committed to improving *with* you.

As we go through each chapter, there will be opportunities for you to answer questions by yourself or together with the person you are dating. I highly encourage you to look at each of these sections and give thorough answers. You'll have some incredible conversations as you do, and you may find out new things about yourself or your relationship. I'm thrilled for you. Let's do this!

Nick

If you're opening this book and you're anything like me, you probably want to know something that will get you ahead, save you time, and hopefully spare you some pain too. I want you to know something up front: this book is not written from a place of relational prowess but out of my own experience walking through a season of failed relationships, until I learned a few things that have led me to a happy, honoring, and life-giving relationship, and now marriage. I wish I could tell you that I got it all right on the front end. I wish I could tell you that I had this information when I was in your shoes. But I didn't. I had to live through the experiences and pain, just like you've probably done, to help me learn what works and what doesn't.

So are we going to ignore the elephant in the room or just let it hang out for a while? Why in the *world* did we write a book on healthy dating and relationships in our twenties? What could we possibly know? Isn't that what the experts with far more life experience and degrees on the wall are for? How could we think that we have been married or in a relationship long enough to have the qualification to write such a book? Those are great questions, and I'd ask those questions if I were picking up this book too. You caught me. I'm not fifty-five and "seasoned." I don't have a host of PhDs, nor am I a relational psychologist. But what I am is a young man who has experienced the world and, through God's grace, learned something about relationships. I've grown up right next to you in this social media age. I've been your classmate. I've seen the world as you have seen it. Let me say this as clearly as I can: I am forever grateful for the men and women who have those degrees and life experiences and wisdom they are willing to pass down to the next generation. I want to make my gratitude for their work known, but I think it is important to realize that sometimes we don't need a PhD; we just need the ear of a big brother or someone who has experienced the world as we experience it. The reality is simply this—this is not the same world our parents grew up in. I think they would acknowledge that too. Whether that is for better or worse, I will leave up to you. Nonetheless, it is vastly different. And the way our culture sees relationships is also different. But some things never change. The desires of the human heart have always been the same, and one of those desires is for peace and joy in our lives, relationships included.

I will do my best to be up-front and honest with you in this book. I'm not going to tell you everything is all right if it really isn't. I'm not going to let you get yourself into a mess if I can help it. I want to save you from as much pain and hurt as I possibly can. I seek to serve you through this book, not direct you. In an age when truth is what you want it to be, when everything seems as if it is based on feelings and doing what our hearts tell us to do, when social media clout is what affords someone authority and expertise, I want to approach this from a different perspective. First and foremost, I want you to know that if you and I happen to have opposing viewpoints on something, I respect you entirely. I welcome you, and I offer you a seat at this table to be part of this conversation—I know, it's hard to have a conversation through a book. But I hope this can be the beginning of dialogue between us. I would love for you to message me on Instagram and continue the conversation we're starting here.

Maybe you and I aren't so different. I've gone through pain in this area of life before. Maybe you have too.

Don't you secretly wish that the skies would part and God would give you a big glaring sign that someone is the right or wrong person for you? I know I did. Throughout my mistake-stricken high school years, I felt a deep sense of disappointment and grief. All around me I saw others in what looked like successful dating relationships. I seemed to be in one short-lived failed relationship after another. They ended for just about any reason imaginable. From things as simple as a girl's dad not really liking me, to things as complex as sexual mistakes we made that caused shame and put our relationship in danger, and just about everything in between.

I wanted nothing more than to find the right person, to know she was the right person, and to live happily ever after with no grief or regret. Sound familiar? What I came to find out in the years to come is that there is no cut-and-dried formula or easy three-step plan to figure out this process. There is no one-size-fits-all dating blueprint. Finding the right person to spend the rest of your life with is not usually something that's simple and easy to understand. In fact, most times it feels like a bit of a mystery. To say that I was frustrated and hurting in this season of my life would be an understatement.

If we're honest with ourselves, we've all probably felt this way at times. For some of us it comes in seasons, and for others it seems to be perpetual and unending. I think the reason so many of us face this same problem of uncertainty and a lack of clarity on how to go about the process is because nobody ever taught us how. Even with advice from others, singleness, dating, and engagement can often feel like a DIY project that you just have to fumble your way through and hope you get right. I distinctly remember sitting at Reveille Café in Marietta, Georgia, some years ago with a mentor of mine who had been married for several years at that point. I remember sharing some of the frustrations I was going through in my relationship, and he shared an analogy with me that I'll never forget. He told me, "Relationships can often feel like trying to get through a maze with a blindfold on." Amid all my frustrations and worries, I felt seen. I felt like I wasn't alone. For the first time, I realized that this is not easy, that it isn't supposed to be easy, and that the pain caused by the difficulty and frustration is very real.

I remember vividly the feeling of immense frustration, not with myself or the woman who is now my wife but with the situation, because it seemed as though there was no clear answer. I loved Chelsea, but how was I supposed to know if I would end up regretting the decision to commit to a life of marriage later down the road? Was I scared of commitment? Was I allowing friends and relatives who would often ask, "So when is the wedding?" to have too much influence in my relationship? Was there something in my past that was holding me back from making a choice? Was it all those things combined? I wasn't sure at the time.

Wherever you are in your dating relationship, this book is for you. From those of you who have been stuck in a place of sexual sin that you cannot seem to shake, to the ones who need a bit more assurance that this is the right relationship and that your significant other is right for you, you've picked up the right book.

If you don't take anything else away from this book, just know this—there is hope. Your feelings may not be telling you the truth. I will never forget a cold night in February 2018, right after Chelsea and I had just gone on a date. We got into a disagreement at dinner that turned into a full-fledged fight in the car. After about five minutes of back-and-forth, I decided to stop talking and not say anything (bad idea). Chelsea sat in the passenger seat as I navigated the dark, rainy roads of northern Georgia back to her home to drop her off. I looked over at her just before we pulled in her driveway, and the tears falling from her eyes glistened in the glow of the streetlight. She opened the door as I sat quietly in the driver seat, leaned toward me, and said, "Just break up with me then," and rushed inside. You know that feeling when your stomach drops and your adrenaline spikes? That is what I felt in that moment. I felt like I was in a daze—confused and utterly hopeless.

Maybe you have felt that way too. How can this relationship that seemed to be working have taken such a turn for the worse? How can I feel so unsure right now? What I learned from a series of failed relationships and attempts to get it right was sobering when I thought about it.

While I don't know of anyone with a story of God tearing open the heavens and writing the answer in the sky, I do know of countless individuals who have searched for these ten things we're going to talk about in the coming chapters—in themselves and in their significant other—and have seen success in their relationships. Some of these individuals were unintentional in doing these things, and some of them were very intentional about having these conversations and implementing a plan in their lives and relationships. I know that when you see a list of ten things, it can seem like the magic formula for making a relationship successful. Please don't misunderstand us—this is not a magic list. This is not some new formula for mastering relationships or convincing someone to fall in love with you. These are ten elements of relationships that, as we have observed, others in happy and healthy marriages get right. This applies to our own marriage as well.

These ten things aren't revolutionary, nor are they brand-new ideas. They are age-old, biblically based, and objectively true no matter what culture says or thinks regarding them. They will be just as true two hundred years from now as they are today. But my hope is that they can be presented in a way that resonates with you, that they aren't just more words on a page. This book is filled with content you can put your hands on, grab hold of, and practice, helping you to make some great decisions for your future and your relationships. These truths are meant to be on the ground, approachable, here for you to get—so you can see your life change as a result. That is my prayer above all else for this book.

Here are a few questions for you to answer for yourself before we continue.

- What do you hope to get out of this book?
- Are you open to having your mind changed?
- Are you willing to make hard decisions if you're convinced they're the best for you and your relationship?

INTRODUCTION

We Never Thought God
Would Tell Us This

Nick and Chelsea

Nick

I think back to a warm, sunny November afternoon in 2016 when I was on the campus of Santa Fe College in Gainesville, Florida. As I was walking back to my car between classes, I sent a DM to this girl named Chelsea that would forever change my life.

I managed to type the message while carrying a hot cup of coffee, doing my best not to run into anybody. I didn't know that God was setting me on a journey that I would never turn back from.

Two days after sending that note, I got on FaceTime with Chelsea for the first time. I was a nervous, awkward freshman in college who had no clue what life would bring. Before long, Chelsea and I started FaceTiming regularly, which led to both of us attending Passion Conference a few months later. We thought we were being under-cover with our feelings for one another, but we learned later that everyone around us could see what God was setting up. During this conference, God clearly revealed to me that Chelsea was to be my wife one day. And not in the weird-boy-from-youth-group kind of way either. Soon after the conference, we began dating. Two years after that, we married. This is the shortened version, but we will share more later!

Chelsea

When I first met my husband, he was a totally different guy than the one I know now. We were so unfamiliar with each other then, especially in comparison with how much I know and love him now as my husband and the father of my child. I'm thankful Twitter first fanned the flames of our love and that we met in person (hallelujah!) a few months later.

God set up our relationship from the very start. At Passion Conference in Atlanta, I lifted my hands to a worship song and broke down in tears after God gave me a message about my future husband. I was told that I was sitting right next to him (Nick). I honestly didn't know how to process that. I knew at that moment that I was into Nick, but I doubted God's voice. *Maybe that was me? Were those my own thoughts?* These thoughts swirled around in my mind until a few days later when Nick and I began to talk about our relationship, and I found out that God had told us the same thing: our next step would be marriage. I barely knew this guy at the time! He was a Southern boy from North Central Florida, and I was a Midwestern girl from Illinois. I know that sounds a little crazy, but God called us together!

From that point on we continued to build our friendship, dated long distance, moved to the same city, and eventually got married. This is certainly not the way it happens for everyone, but it did for us. Still, there were questions we needed to answer and a journey to get to the altar. More to come about that.

Chelsea and Nick

We want to make sure our message and intent for this book are super clear. Our heart in writing this book is to help you:

- Be equipped to successfully engage in the important conversations every couple needs to have before they get engaged.
- Disarm the anxieties that could come with commitment by addressing these ten areas before you get engaged.
- Discover exactly how to dig deep and get honest to deal with real problems and heal what could break the relationship.
- Learn how to communicate with honesty and empathy about the secrets that may have been keeping you apart.
- Recognize the difference between relational issues that can be worked through and relational red flags you need to pay attention to and possibly walk away from.

Addressing the Elephant in the Room

We fully realize that we are still considered "fresh" in marriage, but this book is not marriage advice—for that, we recommend reading books from couples who have been married for thirty or forty years. Instead, this book contains insight into our personal experiences and how we worked through relationship challenges before our marriage. In this book you'll learn the steps to take in dating before you get engaged, discover the right conversations to have before you think about engagement, and address any mistakes or hurt from past relationships. Additionally, you will better understand what marriage is, why God created it, and what you are working toward together. Our desire is that you will know when you are truly ready for the next step and find out how and why to set some specific boundaries (emotional, physical, and spiritual) before marriage.

If you are dating seriously, engaged, or about to be engaged, this book is for you! It is essential that you have a clear view of what marriage is and that you answer some important questions before saying "I do." We pray this book will help you understand the person you love and create a plan for your future together. We believe in you, and we truly want God's best for you!

Heart-to-Heart

We know what it's like to wonder what your future looks like. So many decisions may seem unclear, or you may not know what is worth focusing on in the relationship you're in. Questions may be on your mind about the seriousness of your current relationship, or you may be wondering how to prepare before you enter into your next relationship that hopefully ends in lifelong marriage! Whatever the case, our hearts are with you, and we pray that Jesus guides you into the truth of who he is and what he wants to do in your future. The future may be unclear, but it is not out of control! If you are choosing to read this book, we commend you for even challenging yourself in this way. Most people glide by this phase in life and don't think critically about the person they are and the marriage the Lord could have for them if they leaned into what he desires for their future marriage. But you are someone who delights in preparation, deciding now that you won't be blindsided by the conversations, questions, and situations that arise in the pre-marriage years. Jesus cares for you more than you could ever imagine, and we pray you feel his guidance and affirmation as you read. We challenge you to take these words that are written and weigh them against Scripture, and if anything seems off, please take the Word of God over ours! We speak with experience, but we are still learning and growing with you! Because our dating and engagement season has passed, we would like to walk alongside you as your brother and sister, sharing some wisdom with you in this season. Many books have been written from the perspective of older married couples, and these are so needed, but very few have been written from a younger perspective in this digital age. Chelsea and I are deeply encouraged by 1 Timothy 4:12, which says, "Don't let anyone look down on you because you are young, but set an example for the believers in speech, in conduct, in love, in faith and in purity." We know all too well that this book will live on past our current state of growth and understanding of the Scriptures and character of God. We ask that you extend grace toward anywhere this book might not fully illuminate the heart and character of our God.

We hope this book can be a resource to help you grab hold of what it means to be marriage minded and to see how a shift in thinking in some different areas can set you up for a lifelong marriage that honors God and your spouse. We're excited to join you in this journey.

Nick and Chelsea

#1 CAN YOU COMMUNICATE?

Chelsea

"It's not what you said, but how you said it."

I remember saying these words after Nick and I had gotten into another tough conversation about planning our wedding. We were about three months into our engagement, and it felt like we couldn't catch a break with all the disagreements we were getting into that week. I wish I had a "push to redo" button that week because I felt so defeated. I knew Nick cared about me and the health of our relationship, but we just didn't know how to communicate.

I just wish I could have given myself the advice I know now. Most of our communication mishaps had nothing to do with what was being talked about, but more the way something was being communicated. I didn't know how to express what I felt and what needed to be said. It has taken me years to be clear and kind (most times) in the way I communicate with my husband, and I am a little embarrassed to admit that. Communicating clearly is an ongoing decision I have to make, and some days I wake up with a bad attitude or bleak perspective. Choosing to lean into these feelings (asking, *Why do I feel this way? Where did these feelings come from?*) but also to surrender them to Jesus is a must, and it's not always my first thought to do so. Can you relate?

I've watched from afar couples who seemed to have the communication element of their relationship figured out (or so I thought), but as I asked them questions, I realized that they struggle in this area as well. Most of our relationships aren't lived out in public, and behind closed doors every couple has to learn how to communicate. If you feel like you can't get through to your significant other, or you're afraid you are failing in this area, don't be scared. Welcome the process! Gosh, I wish I would have embraced the hard conversations at the beginning of my relationship with Nick and dropped my pride.

I'm a firm believer the many reasons cited for divorce are not the main problem. If couples knew how to *communicate* about those dividing issues, such as money or commitment or intimacy, I think many more marriages would be saved. So ask yourself this: How is your communication with your significant other? Does it need some work?

I remember having a conversation with our mentors in South Carolina over dinner when we were newlyweds. We looked forward to getting together with them because we always had a ton of questions for them and loved the advice they'd share with us. We asked them how we should handle our communication struggles. Their advice struck us deeply because we realized our focus was in the wrong place. What we were actually struggling with was how we *heard* one another. Have you ever thought you were extremely clear in what you said to someone, but all they heard was judgment or criticism? We realized that our insecurities were causing us to fill in the blanks and hear things that weren't being said. No matter what was spoken, we thought the intentions of the other were rude and hurtful because we were hearing through a filter of defensiveness. I would express that I thought we had gotten into a routine with what we did for fun or for our date nights and that I would like to change it up and do something different that I enjoy. Nick would *hear* that he hadn't been thoughtful enough lately and that he needed to do better. I was hoping that he would hear that it can be easy to default into a routine, so we should switch things up to create new memories and enjoy new things together. But in the moment, he just heard that he wasn't good enough. Has this ever happened to you? The greatest advice we got from that dinner with our mentors was to state the intentions of a conversation before getting into it. So now, whenever Nick or I bring up something we would like to change, we share something like this: "I want to share with you how I feel about something, and I would love if you could be in listening mode instead of 'fix it' mode. I just need to share this with you because I love you."

A lot of guys want to immediately fix an issue, and if they can't, they tend to feel trapped or like they haven't lived up to an expectation they placed on themselves or someone else placed on them. This can be an issue with women as well, but I've noticed it especially with guys. What can be so helpful is disarming that tendency at the start of the conversation. Asking them to listen to you rather than feel they need to fix right away allows for space to just talk. This advice has been so helpful for us in marriage.

Assumptions and Reality

I have failed so many times by assuming the worst about my husband. This habit wasn't formed in our relationship, but beforehand in adolescence. Somewhere down the line in my relationships with family and friends, I saw examples of people holding their promises loosely and not being who they said they were. I started to assume the same of Nick—and I had to learn to take this pattern to God and ask him to change me. If I assumed my husband had bad intentions, it showed in the way I treated him.

Assuming the worst about the one you love will sabotage something good and stop it before it can ever be great.

My assumptions frequently had more to do with my view of men and my past relationships than with anything Nick had said or done. I remember the moment we were having a conversation before going to bed, and God convicted me of treating my husband harshly because of assumptions I held. When the truth hit me, I broke down crying and apologized to Nick for my selfishness. I wish someone would have told me what I was doing before

I recognized it myself. Assuming the worst about the one you love will sabotage something good and stop it before it can ever be great. Ask your person to let you know if they see this habit unfolding, as they might notice it before you do. When you recognize a pattern of assumptions, be honest and admit your inaccurate perspective. This will help you take steps in a healthier direction and improve your communication.

CLEAR COMMUNICATION PROMPTS

This is going to take some work, but it will pay off in your relationship later—trust me! Here are a few questions to ask one another. Set the tone of this conversation by welcoming honesty. There is no room for a defensive spirit. Before you have any important conversation, pray that the Lord would soften your hearts for growth and show areas needing improvement. Ask for solutions and a clear path forward. Let's do this!

Come together and answer these questions freely.

1. In our daily conversations with each other, do you feel you can be honest with me? Why or why not?
2. What does my tone feel like to you when we're having serious conversations?
3. What makes you feel welcome to be who you are?
4. What do you value most in friendship?
5. What do you value most in our relationship?

These are just a few places to start. I can guarantee more questions will arise naturally and this conversation will be a memorable one!

Listen Up

Fools find no pleasure in understanding
    but delight in airing their own opinions. (Proverbs 18:2)

To answer before listening—
    that is folly and shame. (Proverbs 18:13)

Have you ever looked across the way in a restaurant at a couple sitting at the table with their phones in their hands not even talking to each other? I know it's easy to do this sometimes, but I remember looking around in a restaurant while I was in Italy and realizing that every single person was either speaking or listening attentively to their family or friends. I was told while visiting there that mealtime usually lasts several hours and it is considered extremely rude to even have your phone at the table. I believe every culture and person would benefit from a no-phones-at-the-table rule!

When was the last time you listened to someone without immediately thinking about what you were going to ask or say next? Great listeners seek to understand the person they are communicating with before they think of the next thing that should be said. If you can learn to become a listener, then your relationship will improve significantly, and you'll be better off for it.

So what does this look like? I remember when Nick and I first started recording videos together and talking on our podcast. I had been making videos for six years before this, so I was used to talking to the camera and not having anyone talk back. We quickly realized we both tended to talk over each other. We could barely get a word in because we were both super concerned with what we had to say rather than listening to each other, giving it a moment, and sharing thoughts afterward. It sounds so simple, but I don't think this practice is talked about enough.

I know you care deeply about the person in your life, but when was the last time you paid attention to how much you truly listened to them? You start chatting with your significant other, and immediately you get excited about what they are saying and have a thought to share right away. You open your mouth to talk, they haven't finished their thought, but you jump in anyway and offer your opinion. Or maybe you stay quiet, but you stop listening to what they're saying as you think through how you want to respond to what they first said. Listening—truly listening—is a skill, and you will get better as you work on it. Instead of interrupting or formulating a response, focus on what they're saying. As you continue listening, you may even forget your original thought because you're more interested in what your significant other is saying, now that you're actively listening. When they are done speaking, you might need a moment of silence to think about your response, but after doing this several times, you begin to form a habit of listening, reflecting, and then speaking.

INTENTIONAL LISTENING

Can you work on becoming a better listener? Is the person you're dating a great listener? Do they seek to understand you? Do they validate how you feel and what you say by looking you in the eyes when you talk?

Isn't it frustrating when you're sharing something very meaningful to you and the person across from you is scrolling on their phone? This is how it feels to not be heard or valued in your relationship.

Exercise: For a week after reading this chapter, make a note in your journal of what you notice about your significant other or yourself as you intentionally listen. You may discover new things as you work through this. Your self-control is growing too! This skill is helpful outside of your romantic relationship as well. Just think of how valued your friends will feel as you choose to listen intently and wait to say anything.

Have You Seen Them Mad?

My dear brothers and sisters, take note of this: Everyone should be quick to listen, slow to speak and slow to become angry. (James 1:19)

My dad gave me a piece of advice growing up that was super annoying in the moment but that I learned to appreciate as I got older. (I now realize the frustrating things I heard from my parents as a kid were preparing me for trials I would face in adulthood.) My dad told me, when it came to the guys I dated and had an interest in, to make sure I'd seen them at their worst. He said before you marry someone, it is important to see them get angry, frustrated, sorrowful, regretful, etc. Of course, all the happy emotions are important too! But his point was that often when we are dating someone, we can't see past our emotions because we are so infatuated with them and the idea of us together. It's easy for everything to seem perfect if we haven't been with them when life has been tough. We are usually "in love" and ready to take the next step based solely on our feelings, without thinking about how we will feel and what we will do when life throws curveballs.

I knew Nick was not only the right one to step into marriage with but also a consistent friend to me because I had watched how he walked with me through a difficult bout of mental illness. I had previously left my dream college in California, broken up with my long-distance boyfriend at the time, and was going through a ton of fears. Because of all these life events colliding at once, something in my brain flipped, and I experienced a bipolar manic episode. If you're unfamiliar with a bipolar manic episode, I like to describe this way: one minute I felt on cloud nine (so ecstatic that I said things that didn't make logical sense); the next I didn't know what to do with my intense feelings of sadness and frustration. I remember being in the psych unit and receiving letters and phone calls daily from Nick as I was in the process of healing. The fact that I was going through something harsh with my mental health and he didn't run away made me love him even more. However, it is not lost on me that this was incredibly hard for him. I know that he admitted to being confused and unsure of pursuing me while I was so unstable emotionally. But as he prayed and sought the Lord on it, it was clear to him that these were the right next steps. His steadiness in the midst of confusion also made me extremely secure in our relationship. I knew if I ever went through something like this again, he would be there by my side. I believed he would choose to be a loving and helpful friend on the long road it takes to recover from something so difficult.

Often when we are dating someone, we can't see past our emotions because we are so infatuated with them and the idea of us together.

Can you recall any moments when you've seen your person upset but they handled the situation with grace? Have they been sad but were able to push through? Your significant other should truly have a resolve in their heart to support you through your highs and lows, and you should for them too. Look for signs of harshness or bitterness they may carry when you're working through an issue. Have you been able to resolve issues with mutual understanding and change going forward? The biggest thing I would be wary of is holding on to hope that your significant other will change when they show no signs of putting in the work to change an unhealthy habit. These bad habits, sin issues, etc. will be brought into your future marriage. These problems won't be fixed just because you both have rings on your fingers. I encourage you to examine whether there is anything about their communication that frustrates you and keeps coming up in your relationship. Ask them if they are willing to make changes and head in a new direction. Do they follow through with that decision?

As much as these conversations are tough to have, they will be some of your most fruitful. Think about how much your relationship will grow as you choose to work through the tough conversations and have them now versus later! Hard work is often holy work, and it will pay off.

Tone Matters

Finally, all of you, be like-minded, be sympathetic, love one another, be compassionate and humble. Do not repay evil with evil or insult with insult. On the contrary, repay evil with blessing, because to this you were called so that you may inherit a blessing. For,

> "Whoever would love life
>   and see good days
> must keep their tongue from evil
>   and their lips from deceitful speech.
> They must turn from evil and do good;
>   they must seek peace and pursue it.
> For the eyes of the Lord are on the righteous
>   and his ears are attentive to their prayer,
> but the face of the Lord is against those who do evil."
> (1 Peter 3:8–12)

"No, really, I'm fine!" I said in a tone that screamed I wasn't fine.

How many times have I done this to my husband? When would I learn to share the truth immediately? Easier said than done sometimes, right? I could say I'm fine all day, but he always knows I'm not simply by the way I say it.

I'll admit, I rarely thought about my tone with Nick when we were dating and engaged. I've learned to recognize now, though, that whenever I'm saying something in a tone that is dismissive, sarcastic, or belittling, whatever I say is not going to be heard, and we both may get hurt in the process. The goal of the conversation is squashed under the pridefulness of my tone.

Early in dating Nick and I were sarcastic with each other often. It was our way of joking around, and we didn't sense any harm in it. However, after several conversations with our mentors over dinner, they pointed out how harmful sarcasm was to their relationship.

Maybe you're not sarcastic in your relationship, but perhaps one or both of you dismiss the feelings of the other or you are passive-aggressive in your communication. For us, as sarcasm was our weakness, we fought to remove it from they way we talked. Our personal reasons for doing so were that sometimes we misinterpreted the sarcasm as having truth to it, or we believed we were just having fun but ended up with misunderstandings and hurt feelings. Since we've decided to stop this way of communicating, our intimacy has drastically improved. It has only benefited our relationship.

Have the Big Conversations In Person

I gave a big sigh of relief after pressing Send. I couldn't believe I had just broken up with my boyfriend of nearly a year over text. After all, the thought of having that conversation in person terrified me, and I knew I would be too weak to stand firm on my decision if I had to see his reaction. So I shut off my phone after pressing Send and chose to look at the response later, whenever I was ready.

Looking back years later, I see how petty that decision was. My boyfriend at the time deserved a real conversation rather than a big text slammed in his face out of nowhere. My fear of hurting him held me back from an opportunity for mutual understanding. And likely it was as much about my discomfort with the situation as it was about not wanting to hurt him. I realize now that a little bit of growth in the communication department would have done me some good.

There have been countless times when I decided to have a conversation over text that should have been had in person or at least over the phone. Have you experienced this? Maybe a conversation felt like too much work, so you just started rolling out your feelings and thoughts over text message, and it ended up being way more serious than it needed to be or way more drawn out. Gosh, I wish I could have told my former self to put the stinking phone down. Part of this battle, I believe, is a failure to realize that just because something may be hard to talk about doesn't mean it won't benefit the relationship. Some of the most life-giving moments I've had were on the other side of honesty and conflict.

There Is Intimacy in the Conflict

I used to flee confrontation. At any sign of a conversation going in a direction where there might be disagreement or uneasy feelings, I'd walk out of the room or completely shut off. For me, it was a way of coping and protecting myself. I thought the only beneficial conversations to have were those where everyone ended up happy. I had a rude awakening during our engagement season as conflict after conflict arose in areas of family, money, stress, communication, and more. Pretty much every topic brought up in this book was a conflict moment for us at one point. Do you know what I realized after years of deciding not to run from these conversations? Conflict rarely ends in separation if two people are committed to understanding each other. I didn't want to lose Nick through these challenging situations we went through. That possibility scared me, and that is why my first inclination was to run from challenging times. However, after having to press through them, I realized the conflict produced deeper intimacy. I still don't get excited about a heated conversation, but I'm not afraid of conflict anymore, knowing that pressing in will bear fruit if the goal is understanding.

Hard work is often holy work.

Conflict rarely ends in separation if two people are committed to understanding each other.

Journal Prompt: Take a few moments to write out several times you've had conflict in your life. What did it look like? What was your response? Did the end result bring greater understanding of the person you had conflict with? You may see in your examples that you handled conflict differently as a child versus as an adult. That is a good thing to note! As you write, make a separate section of how you would like to view conflict moving forward. I'll show a graph of how I have viewed it in the past and how I view it now.

PAST VIEW OF CONFLICT	NEW VIEW OF CONFLICT
draining	life-giving
scary	an invitation to greater intimacy
What if they don't agree?	What if we understand each other better?

Conflict Breakdown

Looking at this you may think, *How in the world can I get from point A to point B, Chelsea?* I'm happy you asked. If you have viewed conflict negatively in the past, ask yourself why. For example, maybe conflict has seemed draining to you, like it has for me. In my case, the anxiety I felt about conflict caused me to feel drained even more than the actual conflict itself. I worried myself to death before any conversation was had! At this point, if you realize you have deep-rooted insecurities or negative views about conflict, talking to a professional counselor may do you great good! Premarital counseling blessed our lives so much, and we developed confidence in areas where there were misunderstandings at first.

> **I'm not afraid of conflict anymore, knowing that pressing in will bear fruit if the goal is understanding.**

Oftentimes amid conflict, we look to the other person to heal our insecurities. The way to combat this is to ask Christ to fill you with his love, his perspective, and his hope!

There is beauty in conflict when deeper understanding of one another is possible. We can look forward to these moments with the hopeful expectation that God is going to show up and do what only he can do!

A Few Words from Nick

Early in my teenage years I had a mentor who stressed to me the importance of excellence in communication in every area of my life. He said that in his thirty-plus years of pastoring and counseling, 95 percent of the arguments he helped people with could be avoided or worked through quickly if people took the time to improve their ability to communicate.

Much of the time, what I needed to do was develop the ability to listen, and to respond with fewer words and less emotion. There is a place for emotions in communication, but it is vital, as we are working through obstacles in our relationship, to approach the challenge with an objective, levelheaded perspective. The worst arguments Chelsea and I have ever had were when we were both emotional—sad, angry, jealous, and the like. Whenever I overhear couples nitpicking back and forth, I wonder if they are fighting to overcome a problem together as a team or just to prove their partner wrong. All this ever does is further drive a wedge in their relationship. The art of communicating is a powerful tool, but when used the wrong way, it can cause extreme damage.

Have you heard the childhood rhyme "Sticks and stones can break my bones, but words can never hurt me"? I have too, and I think it's incorrect. People have said some really nasty things to me that have hurt me; maybe you've experienced that too. Don't be the person who does that. As humans, we have the gift of being able to share thoughts and ideas and really connect with one another. Steward that gift well, and your relationship and life will benefit as a result.

#2 DOES PRIDE GET IN THE WAY?

Nick

I was sixteen years old, a junior in high school, and I was trying out for my school's baseball team on a warm Florida day after school. I was exceptionally nervous and excited. I remember getting to the field and warming up with some of the guys who had been playing for years. I truly felt like I was better than them in certain areas, even though I had only picked up a baseball for the first time about three months prior. As we went through our warm-up drills, I noticed my partner throwing differently than I was used to. I swiftly corrected him by giving a firm "Clean it up—these throws are useless!" Little did I know, my throwing partner played on the varsity team his freshman year and had nine standing college offers at the time and a private ex-MLB coach. He was doing specific warm-up drills that would help stretch ligaments in his arm throughout the afternoon. Whoops.

As we got into our tryouts, we began by running bases. I nailed this. Next, we moved to hitting. I got compliments from friends who said I looked like I'd been playing for years. To say I was feeling prideful would be a massive understatement. In my mind, I was the top gun on the diamond that day. Then it was time to field—the exact thing I had just "coached" my superathletic friend how to do correctly. Everyone ahead of me had solid fielding technique and great throws back to home plate. However, I felt good; I got up to field the ball, and as it sailed to the outfield, I completely missed it. As quickly as that baseball flew over my head, my hopes of making the team flew right along with it. I began sprinting to the field wall to retrieve the baseball, and as I recovered it and threw it back to home plate, I was ten to fifteen feet off the plate—a total miss. I walked back to the dugout in absolute humiliation, feeling the scorn of those whom I had attempted to instruct. And no, I didn't make the team.

What did I learn that day? My arrogance was repulsive, and I didn't deserve to make the team, no matter how good I thought I was. The Bible talks about this. James 4:6 says, "But he [God] gives us more grace. That is why Scripture says: 'God opposes the proud but shows favor to the humble.'"

If we're honest with ourselves, we all deal with this. Every single one of us. I believe it goes back to the garden of Eden when Adam and Eve chose to believe that their own way was right and good instead of accepting God's definition of what was right and good. There was a decision that came about in the brains of Adam and Eve to say, "We know better, and our choice is the right one, and it is better than God's choice." This is the first time we see the spirit of pride rear its ugly head in the Bible. Why do I bring this up? Because since that day, every single person has been affected by the ramifications of their choice. You don't have to look far to find it: Political parties going for each other's throats because they believe their way is the only way. Church denominations that believe their interpretation of theology is completely perfect, and anyone who doesn't agree is wrong and doesn't know the Bible. Influencers who believe they are more important than someone else because they've built a following. I'm sure you don't have to be convinced that pride is all around us.

So why do I feel a need to talk about this with you, especially as it relates to relationships? Because pride can consume your relationship and lead you somewhere you never thought you'd end up. If you can't yet recognize pride, either in yourself or in the person you may spend your life with, take time to analyze how often motives seem self-seeking. The antidote to pride is humility—our goal is to lead a humble life alongside someone else doing the same. So how do we live amid something like pride and not be overtaken by it or captured in its grips? I love this quote from an unknown writer: "Ships don't sink because of the water around them; ships sink because of the water that gets in them." I would like to add that a person doesn't become prideful because of the pride around him but only when he allows it to get inside him. You can certainly live in the midst of chaos and pride and remain calm and humble. As much as you can, survey the lives of those around you and make sure you're placing yourself around others who are gentle in spirit and humble at heart. We have the option to choose our friend groups. The Bible says in 1 Corinthians 15:33 these profound words that shaped my understanding of this truth some years ago: "Do not be misled: 'Bad company corrupts good character.'" If you are consistently placing yourself in an environment that only feeds and encourages self-centered behavior, you are swimming upstream for no reason, and your relationships will suffer because of it.

I'm sure you can think of moments in your life when you've encountered someone who came off as haughty or arrogant. They might have made you feel small and unintelligent, less than, and not good enough. I know this has been the case for me. I believe that having a humble spirit is not only for our own good but also for the good of those we encounter daily. The humble man or woman is not the perfect individual. They are not without flaws or struggles. They don't hold to a sense of entitlement, nor do they believe that they deserve whatever they wish. The humble one is always looking out for others first and themselves second. They are willing to admit when they make mistakes and don't make excuses for their actions. They have a willingness to apologize directly and ask for forgiveness. They don't seek to impress others based on merit, possessions, or accolades. The haughty live a lifestyle that screams, "Look at me!" and search for validation from others. The humble live a lifestyle that screams, "Look at Jesus!" knowing that he is the source of life, joy, satisfaction, and fulfillment.

I often think of David crying out to God for mercy after being trapped by some of the biggest mistakes one could make. In Psalm

51:1–2 he says, "Have mercy on me, O God, according to your unfailing love; according to your great compassion blot out my transgressions. Wash away all my iniquity and cleanse me from my sin." Do you sense you are living for the approval of others in your life or in your relationship? Maybe spending money on things to impress others? Ignoring character flaws and relational problems as though they don't matter? Maybe refusing to admit when you're wrong? I want you to be brutally honest and not sugarcoat it, because if you do, it will come back to bite you down the road.

When I was growing up, there was one movie series my dad and I would watch every single time we saw it come on: *Pirates of the Caribbean.* The movies were captivating to me from a young age. Maybe it was the romance between Orlando Bloom and Keira Knightley and the willingness to risk life itself if it meant being together. Or maybe it was the determination of Johnny Depp's "Jack Sparrow" to leave behind his failures of the past and walk into the destiny of ruling the seas. Or maybe it was just the age-old pursuit of some lost treasure yet to be found. I think we can all relate to some degree—even if Jack Sparrow isn't your thing, we are all searching for a treasure in this life, aren't we? Maybe it's to be accepted into that school, or to get that car, or to live in that house, or to score that job, or to just get that one thing we've been wanting. I get it. Longing is deeply embedded in the human heart, but what would happen if we took our focus off ourselves and placed it on God and his heart and desires for our lives? We spend our entire lives searching for treasure, when all along the real treasure is the heart of God. Recognizing this truth is a major step in the direction of living a humble life.

Unfortunately, you don't wake up on a Thursday and suddenly become humble. Your only hope of becoming a humble person, or marrying a humble person, is by first being humbled by considering the glory of God. Again and again, I must choose to bow my knee and ask for his strength to guide me into a humble life. When I understand my own personal sin and my need for redemption by a perfect Savior, the way I look at God, myself, and the world around me is transformed. I will begin to blame others less, take more responsibility, and show patience and grace for the mistakes of others.

Why am I taking time in a book on the things you need to know to ensure you've found the one to talk about personal humility and the humility of your significant other? Because I truly believe that this is one of a few areas that you must not bypass or overlook if you are seeking a loving and fruitful marriage down the road. If you don't talk about humility early on with your person, later you may come to find that pride has a death grip around you and your marriage and is squeezing out every bit of life and beauty.

I think you'd agree with me when I say that humility is beautiful. The more life I live, the more I despise my own self-centered pride. What's weird is that we often don't see it in ourselves at first, do we? Just like my baseball story, we all have our own stories of where our self-centeredness got in the way of something God was wanting to do. There is beauty in submitting our desires to his. When two people walk in a harmonious and humble relationship with Jesus and each other, there is so much life and joy to be found. The individuals I know who have had the most challenging time in relationships weren't unattractive or socially awkward, nor did they deal with anxiety or depression. The people I know who've had challenging relationships issues also "coincidentally" have an inflated sense of self and remain in a state of pride and haughtiness before the Lord and others. Don't let that be you!

One of my first jobs soon after I moved away from home was as a hardwood, carpet, and tile-flooring salesman in the Atlanta area. I was about two weeks into the job, and I remember vividly a bitterly cold Wednesday morning in late January when I was late to a 9:00 a.m. meeting. When I arrived shortly after 9:10, my boss approached me and asked me to come into the meeting. I walked in, apologized for my tardiness, and sat and listened and contributed to the meeting to the best of my ability for the next fifty minutes. As the meeting concluded, I gathered my notepad and checked my phone calendar to see when I needed to be at my first sales appointment of the day. My boss approached me and asked me to join him briefly in his office. The next twenty minutes consisted of me getting lectured about how if I were ever late again, there would be severe consequences and potentially an end to my employment. As much as it hurt to hear, I understood. I had been irresponsible and underprepared. For our next 9:00 a.m. meeting, I made sure I was fifteen minutes early. As 9:30 passed on the clock, with the entire staff present, my boss came frantically rushing through the door, fumbling Starbucks in one hand and Chick-fil-A in the other hand. He was quick to apologize, but these instances of demanding responsibility while not modeling it continued in the months ahead. I resigned in May.

I learned something that morning that would forever change my outlook on humility. It is very easy to hold others to a standard that we are not willing to hold ourselves to. To take the high road is to display ownership and humility in such a way that it naturally provokes others to do the same. The culture you create in your relationship is what will carry you in the good times and the bad.

There is no cut-and-dried, black-and-white way to make an assertion or judgment that person A is humble and person B is not. I think it's appropriate that you take up the tougher task of doing two things: look inwardly at your own life as rigorously as you can, and then with a spirit of grace, observe the life and attitude of the one you are considering spending the rest of your life with. However, it is almost always easier to assume or find pride in others rather than in ourselves, and that in and of itself is the spirit of pride at work. This spirit says, "They are worse than I am."

REFLECTION QUESTIONS

Here are a few questions that may be helpful to ask yourself:

- Do I or does my SO (significant other) always blame others for issues or problems?
- Do I or does my SO try to take responsibility for our actions?
- Do I or does my SO listen intently when someone is speaking, or just prepare for what we want to say?
- Do I or does my SO show a willingness to apologize and ask for forgiveness when we are wrong or out of line?
- Do I or does my SO live in a state of feeling like we need to do certain things to impress others or make others think better of us?
- Do I or does my SO view ourselves as better than anyone else in any way?
- Do I or does my SO really believe we need the grace of God to cover our shortcomings?
- Do I or does my SO enjoy feeling like we are superior to others? (I've struggled with this one.)
- Who is the humblest person I know? Would they agree with how I live?
- What changes do I need to make today?

Was that rather difficult? I understand. I have asked myself these same questions, and continue to as often as I can. If you notice something within yourself, or in the life of your SO, that needs to change, sit down and have a conversation about it together and commit to making changes in whatever area needs to be changed. I promise you will never regret it, as hard as the conversation might be.

> Humility is the fear of the LORD;
>
> > its wages are riches and honor and life.
>
> (Proverbs 22:4)

A Few Words from Chelsea

I could give example after example where my own selfishness got in the way of what Nick and I were trying to work through. I specifically remember a time when we were toward the end of a disagreement and a resolution was close, but I prolonged the process by my defensiveness. It's crazy how after most of our moments of disagreement, I can't remember what we disagreed about, but I can remember how I felt. I'm reminded of a frequently quoted saying: "[People] may forget what you said—but they will never forget how you made them feel." I never regret dropping my pride and defensiveness and going in for a hug. Have you ever experienced a hug amid a tough conversation? It always feels incredibly redemptive to me.

Another conversation I remember having with Nick happened one night just before bedtime. We were going back and forth about stress we were experiencing with work and other people, and the problems had nothing to do with our relationship. But in the process of talking things through, we ended up taking out our frustration on each other. Realizing we were doing this, I stopped us both and reminded us that we were focused on the same goal and wanted the same things. I mentioned that we should postpone our talk until the next day because this conversation was leading to stress before we went to sleep. Thankfully, Nick agreed, and we ended up going to bed resolved to chat the next day.

It is a common temptation for each of us to believe that our perspective or mindset is the right one and our significant other is in the wrong. But humility reminds us that we may not be right. There is incredible value in being teachable and admitting our faults. There is hope for us all in this as we look to Jesus. I'm reminded of a proverb:

> Before destruction a man's heart is haughty,
>> but humility comes before honor. (Proverbs 18:12 ESV)

#3 CAN YOU TRUST EACH OTHER?

Chelsea

My mom grew up watching men take advantage of women. In her adolescence she witnessed a teacher take advantage of one of her closest friends and it impacted her *deeply*. To her, men couldn't be trusted because of these experiences. She didn't have many memories of how a man should treat a woman because her dad (my grandfather) died when she was just three. You would figure that someone with a past like this would become bitter. And I did watch her sit in bitterness for a while. But she didn't like how that bitterness ate away at her joy. She made a conscious decision to forgive those who wronged her and her friends, despite how evil their actions were. I've watched my mom come a long way in being able to trust people. I'm thankful to have watched this road to recovery unfold as her daughter. My mom is now one of the most tender and forgiving people I know. A forgiving person becomes that way by experiencing moments when they too needed forgiveness.

Forgiveness Is the
Key to Joy

If you forgive other people when they sin against you, your heavenly Father will also forgive you. (Matthew 6:14)

My mom wishes she could say that it was easy or her first choice to forgive, but it wasn't. She saw others she loved experience deep hurt, so it was a hard choice to forgive such evil actions. She shared with me while I prepared for this chapter that it's still a struggle today for her to choose forgiveness in her marriage, with friends, and with family. Every time she tried to forgive on her own terms without the help of the Holy Spirit, she held bitterness and resentment in her heart. I've experienced the same thing. I wish I could share that forgiveness is an easy road, but imagine how Jesus felt on the cross when so many of the people he loved had betrayed him. He *still* chose to forgive with the weight of the world on his shoulders.

> Then Peter came to Jesus and asked, "Lord, how many times shall I forgive my brother or sister who sins against me? Up to seven times?" Jesus answered, "I tell you, not seven times, but seventy-seven times." (Matthew 18:21–22)

These words about forgiveness spoken by Jesus himself are an amazing picture of how important it is to forgive in all relationships in our lives. Unforgiveness can eat away at any joy and hope you may have for the relationship. So why the emphasis on forgiveness in a chapter on trust? There is a direct correlation because trust can be built over time even when the person you love has messed up and may do so again. The goal should always be improvement; we will never reach perfection.

A forgiving person becomes that way by experiencing moments when they too needed forgiveness.

No doubt you've had many moments in your life so far when you had a choice to forgive or to hold on to hurt. It is so hard to choose forgiveness in a world that tells us we're entitled to everything under the sun. If it doesn't make you happy, drop it, right? But this is a misleading and selfish way to live. There have been many moments when Nick hasn't made me happy, and I've been disappointed, but forgiveness enables us to go on and grow deeper together.

The Illusion of Control

I can recall a time when Nick confessed sin to me out of honesty and transparency, and I was so grateful he did. But my heart was hurt in the process, and I let that hurt turn into bitterness. My lips said I forgave him, but in my heart I hadn't truly forgiven. My actions after the fact showed that I was trying to hold on to any control I could to make sure that he couldn't hurt me again. But what I didn't realize while doing this was that I didn't allow for trust to grow because I doubted that it could. I had a "come to God" moment when I was convicted that I wasn't trusting God with Nick. I had to release the control I felt like holding on to and instead pray over him and our relationship. I knew the Lord could do way more with my release of control than he could while I was holding on to Nick with a false sense of control. On the one hand, it was a relief to release that burden, but on the other, it took a leap of faith to believe that Nick was in better hands through my prayers than my constant correction. Whew, easier said than done. But every time I'm tempted to try to control my husband, I remember this verse:

> Be completely humble and gentle; be patient, bearing with one another in love. Make every effort to keep the unity of the Spirit through the bond of peace. (Ephesians 4:2–3)

Your Past Trust Issues

Reflecting on my mom's path of growth reminds me that trust is a key component in setting the foundation with whoever we spend the rest of our lives with. The truth is, even those we care about very much will fail us. We must remember that we live in a broken world of sinners. And of course, we know that because we know ourselves and our own tendencies. I think of this scripture in Romans when thinking about how we are redeemed by Jesus (thank God!):

> All have sinned and fall short of the glory of God, and all are justified freely by his grace through the redemption that came by Christ Jesus. God presented Christ as a sacrifice of atonement, through the shedding of his blood—to be received by faith. He did this to demonstrate his righteousness, because in his forbearance he had left the sins committed beforehand unpunished—he did it to demonstrate his righteousness at the present time, so as to be just and the one who justifies those who have faith in Jesus. (Romans 3:23–26)

Your past may include heaps of moments when you could have given up on trust in general. I want to sit in this with you for a second because I know it is not easy to forgive and trust again. It takes intentional heart work. In the moments when trust is broken yet again, there is a call to trust in Christ with your life. Our relationship with Jesus is no "one and done" decision. Daily, as we walk through this life, we are beckoned into a deeper, more profound relationship with him. This call isn't the shout of a loud voice but rather a quiet invitation to press in during times of disappointment so that you can experience his closeness and get perspective on the circumstance you face. When you choose to give in to bitterness and the hardening of your heart, it is your own understanding you end up leaning on. Every time I've chosen to give in to this path of following my thoughts and views of a situation, I've been led astray.

In the moments when trust is broken yet again, there is a call to trust in Christ with your life.

If you've had hurtful experiences, you could begin to view every person with mistrust and judgment. It can be exhausting thinking that everyone is out to get you or will let you down. *Breathe* for a second. Think about how much you desire to do this life with like-minded and loving people. Nearly everyone in your life desires that too. Most people do not *want* to let you down or break trust. Especially the person you'd love to spend the rest of your life with. It is possible to separate the past from the present! Your future can still be incredible in spite of a tough upbringing, hurtful actions, or lack of trust in the past.

After struggling to figure out my past hurts from previous relationships, I wanted someone who was a professional counselor and a firm believer in Jesus to help me through my relationship with Nick. I didn't want to bring old patterns into our relationship, so I thought this was a great step in the right direction. One of my first few counseling sessions that I went to individually involved digging up old thought patterns and ways I'd viewed relationships in the past. After a few times of talking through how these past patterns impacted my view in the present, my counselor hit me with a little psychology that blew my mind. I want to share it with you because it may help you like it did me. She shared that a part of the brain called the *hippocampus* operates like a filing cabinet. When it comes to our memories, the hippocampus calls to mind the *most intense* moments of our lives, and the *most recent* first. My counselor shared that if I wanted to change my outlook on the future, I needed to create new and positive memories associated with the things that used to bring me stress.

She advised me to "bookend" certain activities that I'm working toward changing my perspective on. For example, if I'm having a hard time opening up about my feelings with Nick, before he and I have a difficult conversation, I should do something that brings me peace (like reading or dancing to my favorite song) and follow the conversation with another moment of peace. This might sound silly, but it helps to form new and positive memories around things that I used to associate with stress or fear. New positive patterns and memories allow the good to outweigh the bad. This doesn't mean we forget the past, but we work toward creating a new future with our future husband or wife.

On the Same Team

One of my favorite games that Nick and I like to play with our friends is called The Mind. We love this game because you have to work together; no one can compete with anyone else. Either you beat the game as a team, or you go down as a team. I'll spare you all the game rules, but the best part about this game is watching all our competitive friends realize that they can't win by themselves. We all must focus on putting our best forward and working together.

Isn't the hope of marriage to operate as a team? There have been times when Nick and I were not seeing eye to eye and I wished we had a relationship coach or counselor to guide us through the situation. Someone to remind us that *we are on the same team here*!

I played soccer when I was little, and we had a girl on my team who loved playing offense and getting the ball into the goal. She was great at soccer, but after a while, it became exhausting to play on a team where one person hogged the ball the whole time. When we played a team that was better than her and her skill set, we didn't win because we didn't get a chance to play together to defeat them. We would have had a better chance of defeating them if our team could have played as one, but since we were relying solely on her abilities, we were defeated.

When I rely only on my perspective of my relationship with my husband, I am not as effective as we are together. I was always told growing up that if my future husband and I were not better together than apart, then I was marrying the wrong person. I agree wholeheartedly! Have you ever heard the phrase "kingdom marriage"? I love to describe this as a marriage that is set on Christ and on the goals the marriage can accomplish for him. The goal of kingdom marriage is bigger than us. In this season of preparing your heart for a committed, Christ-centered marriage that will last your lifetime, opening your heart to accept a love that goes beyond you is vital!

A Lack of Trust Can Compromise Your Relationship

Nick looked at me one night and asked me to trust him, as I was giving a million excuses for why I had a hard time opening up to him. My problem had nothing to do with him or what he had actually said or done. I was recalling all the times in the past that I had been hurt. I trusted the wrong guys with my fears and past mistakes. I didn't know if I could open up again, risking that what I shared would be twisted and used against me. But this difficulty trusting and being vulnerable started to shift as Nick showed me time and time again that I was safe to share with him.

The Holy Spirit living inside of us can give us peace or insight about the person we are with. We can go through difficulty after difficulty, but the Holy Spirit is our guide through each bump along the way. Pressing into his guidance will lead us to the truth even in our uncertainties! If you are wondering if the person you are building a future and life with is trustworthy, or you need help learning to trust again, press into the Spirit's guidance.

You can trust again even if the past leads you to believe otherwise. Even if your significant other makes mistakes—and they will—if they come to you desiring change for themselves and have asked you and the Lord for forgiveness, that is a sign of growth and should be embraced!

As I was writing this chapter, I felt led to encourage you to do something bold and different that you may have never done before. Because the power of forgiveness goes hand in hand with trust, I believe there may be some unforgiveness that needs to be addressed. You may be curious why this is such a big deal, but even Jesus points to the ruin of unforgiveness in our hearts.

> If you forgive other people when they sin against you, your heavenly Father will also forgive you. But if you do not forgive others their sins, your Father will not forgive your sins. (Matthew 6:14–15)

Whew. That is heavy! But if we are called to forgive even the harshest of situations and people, God will give us the power to do so. He says he will!

> Bear with each other and forgive one another if any of you has a grievance against someone. Forgive as the Lord forgave you. (Colossians 3:13)

Because Jesus forgave the sins of the world, we can forgive one another. This doesn't mean we need to excuse poor behavior or allow a person back into our lives if they have shown themselves harmful, but it does mean that bitterness will no longer live in our hearts because we have set ourselves free of offense through Christ.

Assume the Best about Each Other

One night Nick and I had stayed up super late talking. We were examining the tendencies and assumptions we'd held toward one another when we were in a long-distance relationship. We realized after airing our frustrations that whenever communication lagged, I assumed he wasn't interested in my day or in me at all. I didn't believe the best about him when he wasn't around. In my past relationships,

I did a whole lot of what-if talks in my head. My mind was full of assumptions, and I didn't like the way that felt.

After a while of talking, he looked at me and said, "I've given you no reason to assume these things, so can you take a chance and trust me? Assume that I want the best for you and us because I do!" I felt so awful when he said this because I realized my mind had automatically been defaulting to assuming the worst. I believe the enemy was even planting lies, telling me that my relationship with Nick was not going to last because no good thing lasts forever (lie).

Get Comfortable with Being Uncomfortable

Remember the days when we were kids, excited to take risks? Outside on the playground I would hear boys yelling across the blacktop at each other, daring their friends to do something crazy. As I've gotten older, I've noticed the tendency in me, and maybe you have in yourself too, to desire comfort. I seek out comfort even in the areas where God calls me to challenge myself. I know the spirit in me is willing, but my flesh is weak (Matthew 26:41). This might be controversial, but I believe it to be true: a comfortable life is not a fruitful life.

Every time I have an argument with Nick, I feel an urge to leave the room. Especially in the first couple of years of our marriage, if we had a conflict, I would want out of the conversation. After years of working on that urge and choosing to stay and communicate, I don't have that desire anymore. There will be opportunities for you and your significant other to choose to stay and work on issues that you have, and I encourage you to press through them. They are times of discomfort, but usually on

A comfortable life is not a fruitful life.

the other side you will find deeper understanding and trust. Trust is built through times when trust is tested. Your love will be refined if you choose to commit to mutual understanding and believing the best about each other.

TRUST-BUILDING EXERCISES

Here are some trust-building activities for you and your significant other to try. Doing these exercises with Nick has been so fun and meaningful that we love to look back and see how they built our trust in one another. Feel free to record or take photos of some of these moments to look back on if you want!

- Take turns planning a date night for the other person, without letting them know the plan (include details of what type of conversations you want to have in the car, what type of food you want to try, etc.).
- Write a meaningful letter about how you feel about your significant other. Share your excitement for the future with them and what you have prayed for over time.
- This sounds silly, but it's fun and it works to build closeness and trust! Sit across from one another in the car, over dinner, or somewhere public and have three minutes of eye contact without moving your gaze from one another and without talking.
- Take time to pray for intentional growth in the area of trust for one another. Ask God to reveal areas of opportunity for growth. Have a notebook nearby to jot down anything impressed on your heart.

> - Take out your phones and share the memories you have through photos of your family, friends, or meaningful events that were impactful to you. Share why and when these things happened.
>
> A few of these moments may have been goofy or different than you're used to. That is the goal! I hope these activities challenged you to dig deeper with one another and that they sparked curiosity in you.

How to Know You're Making Progress

I have failed my husband many times before. I've assumed the worst about him, shut myself off from him, and been slow to forgive. However, there has been significant growth as we've learned to trust and forgive again and again. I know you and I will never be perfect in our relationships, but growth is always available. Progress is always possible. You might not realize at the moment that you are learning and growing, but later you will look back and notice the change.

> I know you and I will never be perfect in our relationships, but growth is always available. Progress is always possible.

You may be growing in trust if:

- Your first reaction to a hurtful conversation or confrontation is no longer anger or apathy.
- You clearly communicate your expectations of one another.
- You recognize that the battles you face need to be fought with a humble attitude and a heart submitted to prayer.

- You give your partner the benefit of the doubt in your mind and communicate if any assumption is being made about the other person.

These are just a few markers of growth, and you may notice more.

Praying Together

For the longest time, even after marriage, it felt like Nick and I were growing spiritually individually, but we still felt weird or awkward praying together. For the first bit of time being together, we couldn't get past that discomfort with prayer together. It's kind of like you're working out for the first time in a long time, and your muscles aren't strong, and certain movements feel wonky. But after exercising those muscles and building strength, your body gets adjusted to what used to be difficult. In an area like prayer, distraction and adversity will come. Things will inevitably try to hamper your prayer life or come between you and your future spouse. Prayer is like glue for marriage. Every time Nick and I have felt disconnected, after we pray we gain a new perspective and empathy for one another. We also gain a stronger sense of connection than we had before. But this takes intentionality and commitment! Jesus is our source. If we find ourselves distracted and discouraged, we ask Jesus to cover us and to give us the hope and perseverance only he can provide. After all, his Spirit is alive and active inside of us. All it takes is asking him to help and depending on him for our every need, even if it seems silly or small. He cares and he wants your relationship to grow in him.

As we move along, I leave you with thought:

Though one may be overpowered, two can defend themselves. A cord of three strands is not quickly broken. (Ecclesiastes 4:12)

A Few Words from Nick

If you can't trust your significant other, you probably won't feel right marrying them, or at least I hope you wouldn't. This is why we believed trust to be one of the ten areas of importance when considering whether you've found the one. I can remember going on dates early on with Chelsea where things just felt different. It wasn't as though sparks were flying and the world was spinning a bit faster; it just felt like for once I was sitting in front of a mature woman of God who possessed a character worthy of trust.

In your life and in your own relationship journey, make trust-worthiness one of the things you observe and think about often. Of course it takes time to get to know someone's heart and character, but ponder whether they have shown integrity and a lifestyle worth trusting. If some time has passed and you begin getting the sense that they just might not be in a place yet where they are mature and consistent enough for a serious relationship, I'd make the appropriate decisions in order to move on. But if they have shown good character and trustworthiness, then I would encourage you to stay the course, discerning where God might be taking you next.

Trust is on our list because life can be extremely difficult through-out different phases. In marriage, there will surely be arguments and disagreements over things like how money is spent, how to align your schedules, or even what to have for dinner on Wednesday. At other points tragedy will strike, and you might experience a death of a family member or friend, a business might fail, or a diagnosis you weren't expecting might come out of nowhere. I don't mean to strike fear or anxiety in you, but what I do mean to say is that life will have its hard moments, just like it will have its beautiful moments, and nothing is more important in those moments than to be supported by someone honorable and trustworthy.

#4 HOW DO YOU VIEW MONEY?

Nick

There is an old and widely shared bit of advice often given to young couples regarding four things that need to be talked through and agreed upon prior to marriage. Maybe you already know what they are, but if you don't, the four things are kids, money, religion, and in-laws. Why have these four things been highlighted throughout time as being crucial to get right in the context of marriage? I'd bet it's because people have found out the hard way that certain important things must be agreed upon to avoid constant tension in marriage.

While all four of these areas are very important, only one of them is given frequently as a reason for divorce. You guessed it—money. I don't know what your past is with money; maybe you have a history of being very responsible and making wise choices with your finances. Or maybe some of you have been like me in the past and made some really poor choices with your money. Whatever the case, you can make progress in this area no matter where you find yourself. While I won't be giving you financial advice, I will share decisions that Chelsea and I have made to drastically improve our relationship with money and with each other.

Money and Your Past

I'm so grateful that our past doesn't have to dictate our future. The key words in that sentence are *have to*. For many, their past does indeed dictate their current reality and their futures because they allow it to. When it comes to money, we all have a past. This is deeper than that dumb purchase you made when you were fifteen.

I mean this in the sense that we all grew up with a certain view of money that has shaped how we see it even now. You might have grown up in a household that was always stressed out when it came to discussing money. Maybe a lot of worry, fear, and anxiety seemed to come about when the topic of money was brought up. Maybe there were arguments and fights over finances or spending, causing you to have a distorted view of money today. Maybe you grew up in a home where money was not necessarily a pain point because there was plenty, but your parents' identity was found in their bank accounts, or extravagant spending covered up deep-seated pain from something else going on. Whatever the case, I am certain of one thing: your past has played a role in the way you view money today. You might be very grateful for that, or you might wish you could see things differently.

How you grew up and how you view money today will need to be discussed with your significant other. I grew up in a home where we worked very hard for what we had, and assuming all the bills were paid and there was some extra, we would spend it wisely and modestly on family outings, vacations, and maybe a couple of things we'd been wanting here and there. Because of this, I took on a mentality of "It's only money. We can make more." So in our home, I'm the spender and Chelsea is the saver. I don't think that either one of these, saver or spender, is the right side to be on. I think the perfect place to be is in the middle. There will be more harmony and peace in your home if you can find a good blend of saving and spending—saving and investing for the days to come, and spending modestly to enjoy some of the fruits of your labor now.

The most important thing to remember is that you and your significant other both have a past when it comes to your attitudes toward money. It needs to be talked through, and I say that from a place of experience. Countless arguments over money ended up happening in our home because we didn't understand how the other viewed money, we didn't have a structured plan and budget that we both agreed on, and we didn't have any idea of where the money we made was even going. Address your past with finances, and do it as soon as you can.

Be Content with What You Have

I truly believe the words of Jesus when he said in Matthew 6:21 that "where your treasure is, there your heart will be also." Wherever we find treasure in this life, or whatever we deem to be treasure, our heart will be attached to that. For some it is to appear successful with a large bank account, big home, nice car, and children attending private school. For others it might be to chase and do whatever makes them happy. At different points in my life, I can definitely say my treasure was not obeying and finding my joy in Jesus; it was money. The problem with money is that it works well to serve humanity, but it does not seem to work well when humanity serves it. Let me be as straightforward as I can possibly be. If you focus all your time, energy, and effort on simply making the next dollar, you will waste your life and end up unhappy.

The longer I have spent thinking about, praying about, and researching relationships and money, the more I've found that our culture tends to have one major issue staring us in the face, myself included at times: greed. We simply crave more than we need. We desire extravagance. We want the best clothes, the nicest home in the nicest neighborhood, the best and most expensive car. I personally don't believe there is anything wrong with owning nice things, as long as they can be paid for outright (with the exception of a home). What I have seen happen over and over again, though, is that couples will immediately stretch themselves far too thin on mortgage payments, car payments, credit card payments, and just about every other kind of payment you can imagine. This eventually leads to financial instability that then stresses and harms the relationship long-term. I would be remiss if I did not remind us both that the end goal is not more stuff; it is a heart that is content and joyful regardless of what is in your bank account or driveway.

Can you be just as thankful and happy to drive a 1994 Ford Explorer as you are to drive a brand-new BMW? Can you be just as happy to live in the $100,000 home as you are to live in the $4.5 million home? Being content doesn't mean you are wrong for aspiring to work hard and build wealth. But seeking material things simply because you believe they will increase your level of joy is wrong. In your relationship, nothing will put you and your significant other on the same page with money faster than if you both agree to be content with what you have, spend less than you earn, be generous, and seek joy in Christ and not in more stuff, no matter how nice or upscale it might be.

What about those, though, who feel like they don't earn enough or have enough to get married and live at peace relationally? I don't believe there is a specific amount you need to make to be happy or to have a peaceful marriage. For some, that threshold is $35,000 as a household; for others, it might be $280,000. Both are completely fine, but what often happens is that the couple who makes $35,000 tries to live like they make $50,000, and the couple that makes $280,000 tries to live like they make $400,000. This is where you will run into trouble if you're not wise and on the same page with the way you budget and spend your money. If you seek to raise your standard of living, make sure you have the means to afford to do it and that you agree as a couple that it is the wisest choice and the best possible way to steward your finances.

In June 2019, we had been married only a few months and were both really stressed about our finances. We didn't know up from down as it related to money. It seemed as though we made money, but we didn't know how much, and when we'd check the bank account, it would be pretty much gone—and so the cycle continued. We sat down one night, emotional but calm, and talked about wanting to change our habits and our treatment of money. We knew from our premarital counseling that this was one of the areas that was important to get right. We held hands and prayed, asking God for his covering and for his guidance as it related to money. We got on the same page about one thing pretty fast—we both hated debt. We knew we didn't want to be "normal" and have boat loads of debt. We knew we wanted to be debt-free, so that was our first step. We began using just a white sheet of printer paper to map what we had coming in, how much we spent on rent, food, utilities, etc., and how much debt we could get rid of every month. Within six months, through diligence, some hard decisions like selling a pricey car and buying a less expensive one, and cutting up our credit cards, we were debt-free. We didn't know it all, but we made progress with what we had. With money, don't feel like you have to know everything before you begin.

Debt

When I was twenty-two, I desperately wanted to finish college and get my undergraduate degree. I saw that I needed about $15,000 to finish up. I looked at my bank account, and to my complete and utter shock, there wasn't $15,000 sitting there waiting for this moment. So what did I do? You guessed it. I logged into my school portal, took out $15,000 in loans in about ten minutes' time, and I was well on my way to my degree. I felt great, I had what I needed to finish, and I excelled through my coursework over the next year, forgetting all about those loans. I walked the stage at Liberty University as magna cum laude, and I was proud of my accomplishment.

I drove back home, framed my diploma, and hung it where I could see it every single day in my office. About a month later, I got a bill in the mail from my student loan agency. Not to worry though—it could only be like a $30 monthly payment, right? Wrong. My minimum payment was $300 a month. I froze in panic, not sure how I would make this work in light of my other monthly expenses. I remember sitting on the couch with my face in my hands, wondering how I'd pay for the decision I'd made over a year ago because it was "convenient." Over the next six months, I looked at that degree on the wall every day and was reminded of my decision. I had a shift in my thinking when I saw my degree as a ball and chain that was holding me back from my future. The same thing for the car in the driveway with a payment on it. The same thing for other stuff I had decided to go into debt over because I "had to have it right now."

Chelsea and I definitely didn't figure this out overnight. The process of learning how to handle money was long and arduous. We found some individuals who were financial experts and listened to them every chance we got. We began to implement what we learned. I was forced to learn how to budget, track expenses, and of course increase income as the provider for our family to get ourselves out of the mess I had made by choosing what felt good in the moment. It wasn't easy or simple, but we devised a plan and followed it. Saying no to things it would've felt a lot better to say yes to in those moments was difficult, but it was worth it in the long run.

In our culture today, it is easy to take out loans on just about anything. Some people are very comfortable with the idea of having debt, while others are not at all. Of course, there are some purchases that the average individual, couple, or family cannot make without a loan, such as a home. However, Chelsea and I view debt as an unnecessary risk that we seek to avoid as much as we possibly can. If I make $4,000 a month, and I have a $1,400 rent payment, a $400 car payment, a $150 furniture payment (yes, this is a thing), a $350 student loan payment, all my utilities averaging about $200, groceries at $600, and insurance payments of $350 to $500 a month, on top of miscellaneous purchases (subscriptions, coffee, etc.) averaging about $250, what am I left with? About $250 in total. That's with no savings and no investing of any sort. Is this the kind of life you really want to live? Stretched thin, stressed out, and overwhelmed by the thought of not getting ahead at all? Now, if you didn't have the debt from the car payment, furniture, and student loan, you'd have about $1200 left over every month to save and invest.

That's a lot of numbers, I know. If your head is spinning a little, that's okay. My primary goal here is to get you to think differently regarding debt. Even if it feels like you're getting ahead of the curve now, you will pay for it later. If I could have a do-over, I would avoid credit cards, student loans, and car loans at any cost necessary. I would happily drive an older car, save up to afford my schooling, and use only money I earn rather than credit cards. The time it took to dig myself out of that hole, and the pain of learning those lessons the hard way, could have easily been avoided if I'd had someone to help me see the consequences prior to making those choices. If you do find yourself in debt now, outside of owning a home, I'd encourage you to realign your priorities and seek to become debt-free or as close to debt-free as you possibly can. Additionally, it is paramount that you and your significant other have discussions regarding debt and how you feel about it. I will never say that you should leave someone because of financial mistakes they might have made. We have all made them. But I will say that you should leave someone who is continually irresponsible and unwise in their financial decisions going forward. This is also a gut check to make sure *you* as the reader are making wise decisions as well.

Generosity

One of the most underappreciated components of money is the possibility for generosity. I remember so vividly the first time Chelsea approached me about a giving opportunity for us as a family. If I told you I was excited about that idea, I would be lying to you. I cared more about the state of my bank account than whether some desperate family on the other side of the world had food to eat and clothes to wear. I was the absolute definition of self-centered and prideful. Today, we give to several different organizations as well as our local church, and although the selfish part of me still cringes a bit seeing those charges hit our bank account, the joy that I have in my heart knowing I'm helping to play a part in true life change around the world and in our community squashes those selfish feelings instantly.

It wasn't just one conversation we had and then the next day I suddenly woke up bursting with generosity. I had to stop and examine what was going on in my heart to gain an understanding of how I saw my finances. What I discovered is that I trusted myself with my money more than I trusted God with my money. I held on to every dollar and cent as tightly as I could because I was scared that God would not come through and fulfill his end of the deal as my provider. How foolish I was. This is exactly why I believe Jesus says these words in Matthew 6:24, "No one can serve two masters. Either you will hate the one and love the other, or you will be devoted to the one and despise the other. You cannot serve both God and money." This verse is *not* saying you can't go to work and make money to provide for you and your family and spend a little bit on nice dinners and gifts here and there. What it *is* saying is that there is no way under the sun for you to have two masters sitting on the throne of your heart. Jesus will not share his throne with anyone or anything, especially a form of currency. It is Jesus, or it is something else, but not both, and the choice is for you to make. He offers you the dignity to have a say in the matter.

Whatever your current thoughts and feelings are surrounding giving, I encourage you to move toward a life of generosity and away from a self-centered, consumeristic culture. Not only for the good of others, but for your own good as well. A mentor of mine, Clayton, once told me something that has stuck with me since the day I first heard it about ten years ago: "God does not want to get the money out of your pocket; he wants to get the greed out of your heart." I hope that rather than considering this component of the chapter a nice little encouragement to give a couple of bucks here and there, you will choose to be a radical giver. If you attend a church, begin giving 10 percent of your income to your church, and beyond that 10 percent, to trustworthy organizations as well. Choose to be generous, and watch God provide in a way that only he can. If I have learned anything at all about money, it is that God will always keep his promise to provide. There was one instance where God really had to show up for me on this, though, because I had begun to doubt if we should tithe that month based on our projected income versus our expenses. Chelsea and I sat down together and prayed about it. We weighed out the pros and cons of our tithe and debated whether we should instead use that money for bills that would come due that month. We didn't feel right about withholding our tithe, but I really didn't think we were going to make it through the month without having bills come overdue. Not surprisingly, God had other plans and reminded me that all money is his money and he can do whatever he wants with it. So we stepped out in faith and gave our tithe, even though the numbers didn't make sense.

A few days after this decision, I received a text from a friend I hadn't talked to in a few years, asking me if I'd be interested in taking on a part-time project with a ministry I have long admired. I assumed it was a volunteer role and nothing further. Long story short, it was a fantastic paying part-time job with a wonderful organization, and it paid more than double what we needed to fill that month's financial need. We chose not to cheat God of what belonged to him, and he chose to honor our faithfulness not only with more than what we needed but also with a great mentorship and relationship opportunity. God will always come through—no matter how much you might struggle to believe it.

Investing and Saving for the Future

The topics of investing and saving are vastly important in a healthy relationship with money and with your spouse. I understand how these concepts can seem a bit disconnected from this book's theme of being marriage minded, but I promise they are not. Maybe you grew up in a household where your parents taught you quite a lot about how finances work. My parents attempted to show me, although I wasn't really interested in what they had to say at the time. Looking back now as a twenty-four-year-old, I wish I'd listened and started learning and investing earlier. I won't be giving you any specific advice on how you should invest your money; however, I do believe you should begin your journey of learning more about it, things like which kinds of accounts would be most beneficial for you and your goals and how you can begin right where you are regardless of your income.

Some years ago, I thought investing was only for people born into great wealth or for those earning extraordinary incomes. I was wrong. I thought investing was something where I could make a million dollars in a year if I invested in the right things at the right time, and while this by a technical definition is true, it is next to impossible and extremely unlikely. In your relationship with your significant other, I would encourage you to begin developing a well-rounded understanding of what you will do as a couple to secure yourselves and your future by leveraging the benefits of investing. You will not regret it.

Combining Your Income at Marriage

One last and rather quick point to make here on this topic is that of combining your finances at marriage. Should you do it? Absolutely you should. If you are entering into marriage, you are combining every part of your lives and making a covenant with your spouse as well as with God. It is wise for you to be working on the same team rather than separately. A study from CNBC shows that married couples who combine their finances have a higher rate of staying together versus couples who continue to keep everything separate.[1] When you get married, make sure that one of the first things you do is go to the bank together and open one joint checking account for spending and one joint savings account that you both have full access to. Committing to a marriage indicates complete and total trust, and your decision making should reflect that choice.

REFLECTION QUESTIONS

- How does your past or your upbringing affect how you view money today? Do you think the two of you deal with money differently? Why?
- Do you have any debts right now? Be honest with your significant other about your finances before you get married.
- Are you committed to a life of contentment with money, or do you believe that more money means more happiness?
- What does it look like in your mind to commit to investing and saving for your future as a family?
- Are you willing to budget in a way you both agree on, spend less than you make, and save up for things like cars, vacations, and other personal wants rather than taking out loans (with the exception of a home)?

A Few Words from Chelsea

My parents grew up in very poor households, raised by single mothers. They watched their moms struggle to make ends meet all while taking care of the kids too. There was constant stress around finances and never a feeling of contentment. The topic of money brought up fear and lack. So stepping forward into adulthood, when my parents started making more money than their parents, they formed a habit of credit card use. They didn't want to experience the feeling of lack they'd had growing up. Ultimately, though, the use of credit cards put them in too much debt. They wouldn't be upset about my sharing this, as they are debt-free now and spending much less than they used to, but they do regret many of their early financial decisions. Thankfully, I was able to learn from their experience.

Money tended to give me a feeling of fear because I had seen it as a fleeting resource in my family. I thought it was money that was causing the issues in our home, but it was actually the stewardship of it. One minute we had money; the next it seemed to be gone overnight from bills. Thankfully Nick and I have worked hard to break down our past with money and build our vision for the future for ourselves and our children. If I could give my younger self advice that I had to listen to, it would be to get on a budget and stick to it. A budgeted life is a life of freedom, not restrictions. Instead of our money having a hold on us, we tell it every month where it's going. For me, this brings so much more peace to my life and marriage.

#5 DO YOU KNOW THEIR FAMILY?

Chelsea

It was a brisk morning in Troy, Illinois, as I was packing up the last few items in my suitcase. Nervousness and excitement pulsed through my body as I thought of what it might be like to meet the parents of my boyfriend. *Will they like me?* I thought to myself as I zipped up the side of my suitcase. *What if they think I'm not enough for their son? What if they don't like my personality? What if they don't like that I'm from a small town in the middle of nowhere?* Worried by all the possibilities of their perceptions, I hopped into our family car with my dad, and he drove me to the airport. This was my first time flying to Florida to be with Nick and the first time meeting his family. Nick and I had met halfway in Georgia several times, and he had come to visit me and my family in Illinois, but this trip was new and daunting in a way. I was especially nervous about meeting his mom. Nick is the youngest sibling in his family, so I knew that he and his mom most likely had a strong bond. The Lord's words to me that Nick and I would one day marry echoed in my mind as I thought about meeting my future husband's family. I knew his family was different from mine and his background different from the way I'd been raised. I just hoped they would accept me and like me. That was all I wanted.

Know Where They Came From

I'll never forget meeting Nick's mom. "Nice to meet you, Mrs. Hurst," I said as I embraced her in a hug. She was a petite woman with short, light brown hair and brown eyes. After a few moments of exchange, I noticed a thick Southern accent. She talked the way I had heard

Southern moms talk in the movies. I just wanted her to keep talking so I could listen to her. I wasn't used to hearing new accents much, as people from the Midwest have more of a flat accent (at least to me). She carried herself with confidence, and she talked about Nick's upbringing and her being the mom of two boys. She had a unique spunk to her, and it was easy to laugh at her quick wit. I saw where Nick got his personality from, and it was fun to watch and listen.

After meeting Nick's mom and dad, I realized something his family valued highly. As they described the harsh conditions of setting tile and hardwood in the houses around North Central Florida, I could tell they were cut from a different cloth. They loved to work hard. Not just any work, but tough and long manual labor in the heat. I was visiting in the middle of the summer during the blueberry season on their farm. Not only did they have a flooring business, but they were farmers as well. There were acres of berries to pick and tons of weeds to pull on this particular visit to their house, as well as jobs to do early in the morning for their flooring business. During my stay, I watched how Nick's dad loved spending time with him in the field. We picked berries during the day and dropped them off at the berry sorting facility at night. It was long and intense work, and I was only there for a week! I had never seen people work so physically hard in my life. I was used to seeing my dad work hours every day on a computer for his job, and now I was seeing Nick's dad and mom work long hours in the heat outside for theirs. I loved that they put so much effort and excellence into everything they did. I saw how this work ethic translated into the way Nick worked on his own jobs and even the way he approached dating and our relationship. I'm so grateful for the upbringing he had. Not to say it was perfect. Every family has issues that they work out, but I appreciate the work ethic instilled in him from childhood.

Soon after getting to know his family, I had a pivotal conversation with Nick that would change our perspective on marriage moving forward. In our premarital counseling sessions, we got to the family portion of our talks and were *floored* by the differences in how we were raised. We compared the way we experienced childhood, the way we perceived arguments, and our communication styles. Our counselors said something that would change our mindsets for the rest of our lives. "As you guys evaluate your upbringings, remember neither of your families raised you a 'better way.' You both have had unique experiences that will benefit your marriage moving forward as you figure out how *you* want to function in your marriage together." There is nothing better about how Nick grew up, and there is nothing better about how I did either. We both let out a sigh of relief as we thought about our futures being paved by our own decisions together that we had control over.

As much as we had control over the way we wanted to pursue our future together, I couldn't ignore the past that Nick came from or that I came from. Our families shaped who we are and our tendencies in many ways. They shaped how we view the world, each other, children, friendship, money, and so much more! At the very least, we needed to acknowledge *why* we say and believe what we do, and we needed to learn how to merge what we'd been taught and what had been modeled to us into our own new family. This process is not seamless, and it's not always pretty, but it has been so important for the health of our relationship. If you and your significant other come from different backgrounds, welcome to the party. The question to ask to help you decide if marriage is your next step is this: What will the future of our family look like given our different upbringings?

I want to give you a chance to begin answering the above question for yourselves. To answer this big-picture question, I find it helpful to answer specific question prompts. I always find specific question prompts helpful. After each question, you'll have an opportunity to write a **charge statement**. A charge statement is something you both agree on to move you forward in your relationship. Chat through the questions together and write your own charge statement that expresses the challenge you will embrace. It doesn't have to be deep or poetic; just make it honest. After the statement, you'll share possible roadblocks in your way so you can work on a solution! You can write these either here in the book or in a separate journal, so you can work individually or together on what you want to say. I've provided an example.

1. How did you see your parents communicate growing up? What kind of communicators do you both want to be?

   Charge statement: *We both will carry honesty into every conversation knowing that our desires are to be understood and to be on the same team. We will do this through clear communication, leaving no room for assumptions or passive-aggressive attitudes.*

   Roadblocks and solutions: What happens if we get mad? We give each other a little bit of space. For us, it's thirty minutes. After a bit of space, we come back together, hug (because hugs rarely allow arguments to continue) and talk it out.

2. How often will you see each other's families?

   Charge statement:

   Roadblocks and solutions:

3. How will you communicate disagreements?

Charge statement:

Roadblocks and solutions:

Hopefully after writing out and sharing these thoughts and statements, you'll feel empowered to work together to address some things that can be hard to talk about. You can put this exercise into practice for more than the questions listed above. You can write your own questions in a separate journal to use whenever you are wanting to learn more about each other and decide how you will champion one another.

God has a funny way of pairing people together. Nick's family is completely opposite of mine in so many ways, and it's almost comical thinking that we ended up together. One of the biggest things to consider while examining the heart of the one you desire to marry is how they were raised and who their family is. I'm not suggesting you say goodbye to them if their family is different from yours or if they (or you) came from a tough home life; I'm simply acknowledging that our family shapes a lot of how we think and what we believe about the world. Some of the most important conversations you'll find yourself having are those that reflect on your childhood and the way you see your future marriage going because of what was modeled to you. These conversations could involve your views of marriage, God, children, work, rest, finances—the list goes on! The prompts above and the diagram you'll fill out in a few pages will help bring clarity to the direction you both want to go.

The Two Become One

The question to focus on through these pages is, How do I know I've found the one? A major quality I looked for in Nick was whether he is willing to die to himself in the same way Jesus gave himself. This is a heart posture that develops throughout a person's life, but it will be evident from the start if it's there.

When we think of Christ and his sacrifice for our sins, we realize there was a price to pay. There was death so there could be new life. This new life is found in the resurrected Jesus, whom you and I may follow today. Thinking of his astonishing sacrifice is humbling and challenging. Have you ever thought of marriage in the same way? What if we viewed two becoming one as an opportunity to discover new life that Jesus is continually creating in us? Marriage is a call to rely on the grace of God that lives in each of us as he molds us together into a new creation. Anyone else envisioning a picture of a three-stranded rope? It won't be easily broken thanks to the Holy Spirit that dwells in us. When you're dating, some key qualities to look for in someone are humility and the fruits of the Holy Spirit actively working in their life. As you think of who you're dating, do you see this in them? In yourself?

> **Marriage is a call to rely on the grace of God that lives in each of us as he molds us together into a new creation.**

As Nick and I shifted our focus from being single and valuing our parents' opinions over each other's to becoming *one*, we each had to learn what it would look like to become our *own family*. We had to learn together how to put one another first before our parents and their thoughts on every move we made while also honoring and respecting them. It took a while for us to break away from how we did things with our families and move toward how we do things together as our own family. When you've talked about your relationship, can you tell if there is any unhealthy attachment to family? For example, do they look for approval in their everyday decisions from their parents or siblings? Do they have healthy boundaries with their family? In Scripture, there is a chapter that talks about the unity within marriage and what it looks like to start your own family.

> But for Adam no suitable helper was found. So the LORD God caused the man to fall into a deep sleep; and while he was sleeping, he took one of the man's ribs and then closed up the place with flesh. Then the LORD God made a woman from the rib he had taken out of the man, and he brought her to the man.
>
> The man said,
>
> "This is now bone of my bones
>   and flesh of my flesh;
> she shall be called 'woman,'
>   for she was taken out of man."
>
> That is why a man leaves his father and mother and is united to his wife, and they become one flesh. (Genesis 2:20–24)

Pay attention to that last verse. Becoming one with another person is becoming a new person. There is a breaking off from the family and unification between husband and wife. It is a beautiful picture, but sometimes the process isn't easy. Because it isn't a walk in the park to die to self, do you see the capability in your significant other to do this? It is hard to become new when you're attached to old ways.

Becoming one with another person is becoming a new person.

When Nick and I got married, we set the expectation early on in our marriage that we were our own family now and the words from our siblings or parents were no longer held as high as we held each other's thoughts and perspectives. I'm so glad we did this early on because it has set the tone for how our parents, siblings, and friends treat us.

I know you are not married yet, but as you think of your significant other becoming your future spouse, they will start to (and continue to) come first as you work to unite and eventually say, "I do."

I know this might be a hard transition for some, and it was for me. My parents did not agree at first with our getting married so young. They worried about how we would be able to make it on our own after only being out of the house for a few years individually. They worried we were moving too fast, sharing that we hadn't thought about finances, and they doubted that **It is hard to** the both of us would finish our educations. **become new when** However, we knew that the Holy Spirit was **you're attached** calling us to marriage and he would provide **to old ways.** a path for us to take as we sought his wisdom from wise counsel, Scripture, and the church body. We put our faith not in ourselves or our families but believed that God would provide a way if we put our hands to work and prayed fervently. He not only provided a way, but we were able to start off our marriage prioritizing each other first, over the opinions of friends and family.

Communication Is Key

I grew up in a family that told one another we loved each other often, gave lots of hugs, and was very expressive. Nick grew up in a family that valued these things as well but primarily showed each other that they loved one another by doing things for each other. As I shared, the first time I came to visit his family, it was the middle of blueberry season on their farm, and they needed all hands on deck to get the berries picked, cleaned, and sent off on the trailer to be eaten by families around the world. There wasn't a lot of time to get to know his mom or dad as they had to focus on work when I came to visit. It was a big shock to me at first that his dad was a man of few words, while my dad could talk for days about a dozen different things. Our families were just different, and we've since grown to really love them, including the unique ways that we learned to give and receive love.

In the beginning stages of our relationship, I was used to expressing how I felt through words and physical touch, while Nick was used to showing me how he felt by doing something for me. We had to learn how to speak each other's "language"! We have since realized that we both really appreciate clear communication.

How Different Families Communicate

Have you ever heard the phrase "To be clear is kind"? I know that Nick feels loved and respected when I am clear with my expectations of him and up-front with how I feel. We've stopped a whole lot of assumptions by this simple principle. I know it may feel like I've shared a ton on communication, but when family gets involved, it can feel extra tough to clearly share the expectations and boundaries you have as a couple for the health of your relationship.

We can't always expect our families to be clear with us even if we are. Often our parents, siblings, and family members have already solidified how they communicate with each other. Even with this being true, deciding to be courageous and confront an issue right away rather than ignoring the problem or downplaying how you feel can change the direction of how you communicate with one another moving forward. Just as in our relationship we don't expect our partner to be a mind reader, we can't expect our families to be mind readers either!

As we think and pray on how to handle each other's families, reflecting on the highs and lows of our past can help us move forward in health. Here's an exercise that we found really helpful: take time to write out key things you remember about your childhood, how your parents communicated to one another, and what you liked about your upbringing. From these topics alone, you will see a tremendous opportunity to learn, empathize with one another, and to pray about your future family and the impact your potential future marriage will have on generations to come. See below for the family breakdown.

THE FAMILY BREAKDOWN		
	HIS	HERS
Childhood memories		
How your parents communicated		
What you liked or didn't like about your upbringing		

Do you see any similarities? Bold differences? After completing this exercise, you may find that the charge statements from a few pages ago may need some revisiting. This is a good thing! Allow for this to be an opportunity for rich conversation.

If Family Is a Sore Subject

Family isn't meant to be a heavy burden, but it can feel that way if there have been hurts associated with one or more of your family members. It can feel difficult to believe your future marriage could be different for you if all you saw was hardship and strife. If commitment was held loosely, it can feel like that will be your story too. But you know what is beautiful about your future? You are choosing to be intentional about setting a firm foundation. You are looking out for red flags and how you can be healthy relationally long term. More questions come to mind that I truly believe will benefit you and your future as you sit and ask these to one another. These will most likely be questions that are also brought up in premarital counseling if you choose to do that before marriage. We did, and it helped us feel ready for the next step.

REFLECTION QUESTIONS

- What were the marriages like in your family?
- What did you see modeled that you liked? Didn't like?
- What role did faith have in your family, and how was that lived out?
- Are their difficult relationships with your family that we should discuss?
- How about holidays and traditions? What's important to you?
- How does your family communicate when there are problems?

You may have found out in this area of discussion that more ground needs to be covered and even more questions come up. That is perfectly fine and to be expected. You may have been a bit uncomfortable bringing up these conversations, and that is okay! Better to be uncomfortable now, before you make a lifelong commitment to someone when you aren't sure where they stand or where they come from. As we wrap up our family chats, let's look at all we accomplished.

We:

- Asked each other about our upbringings.
- Decided what we liked about our childhood.
- Decided what we didn't like about our childhood.
- Analyzed how our parents/caretakers communicated.
- Made charge statements about what kind of communicators we want to be.
- Had intentional dialogue around what it looks like to become our own family.

I pray you feel like you're making ground in how to know if you've found the one you want to spend the rest of your life with. These are deep and thought-provoking conversations to have, but they are vital to the health of your future! One of the biggest blessings you can give yourself and your future spouse is to be honest about your family and upbringing, and how you see these impacting your future together. You can change your future by what you choose to say and do *now*.

A Few Words from Nick

Chelsea mentioned toward the beginning of this chapter that we had grown up in different parts of the country, and with that came a different kind of culture. What I've noticed over the years of us being together and meeting people all over the place is that family structures and upbringings can be vastly different not only from one state or nation to another, but also from the other side of town too. When I met Chelsea's family, they were almost the complete opposite of my family and how I grew up. I was raised on a farm out in the country with tractors, trucks, and dirt. When I arrived at Chelsea's house for the first time, I found it was in a suburban neighborhood with paved roads, and there was a Corvette in the concrete driveway—very different.

What is important to recognize here is that differences are not a bad thing—they can be a great thing. I watched my dad work hard with his hands for twenty years. My now father-in-law works hard with his head. My mom was a solo entrepreneur while my mother-in-law was a grade school teacher. A family structure is important to understand when it comes to your partner—it played a major part in shaping and forming them. However, one of the benefits I didn't know that I'd find, and that you will find as well, is that whenever we put time into understanding how our partner's family dynamic operates, we can have empathy and compassion for behaviors that irritate us but we know were formed in their upbringing. When Chelsea and I started dating, I would often unintentionally hurt her feelings by being very forward and direct with her—not rude but direct—because that's how my family was, and still is. On the contrary, I would often get very annoyed with Chelsea on some of our date nights because she was exhausted and would ask to go home so she could go to sleep. Was I boring? What I didn't know is that Chelsea was committed to her craft and her audience online. She would stay up all night and into the early morning editing her videos for release on her (now our) YouTube channel. Why did she do this? Because it was the work ethic she was instilled with in her upbringing. In the times that you feel yourself getting frustrated or irritated at the one you love, remember it could be part of their formation and how they were taught to see the world. Then understand that in the context of marriage, there is room for you to adjust to each other in ways that will bring about the kind of life you want to share.

#6 WHAT ABOUT SEX AND PURITY?

Nick

I remember it like it was yesterday. It was late winter of 2015, and I was about to enter my senior year of high school. I was excited to see the end of my time in high school approaching, but what I was even more excited about was the girl I had just started dating. We would talk around the clock, into all hours of the day and night. I found myself distracted at work, at school, and just about anywhere at any time. If you asked me then, I would've told you that I'd fallen head over heels in love.

We had assured each other multiple times that we wanted to honor one another and honor God with our boundaries, our purity, and our entire dating relationship. Some months went by in our relationship, and things were going well. We would talk and hang out often, and our conversations were full of depth. Soon though, things went off the rails. We began blurring the lines, crossing boundaries, and making mistakes that we had always swore we wouldn't. The conviction overwhelmed me like I had been hit by a truck. I was in the fullest sense heartbroken, and not over what anyone else had done, but over what I had done. I knew God had more for me and, respectfully, for her too. We soon ended our relationship and moved on.

What did I learn? Through this pain, I learned that God's design is for sexual behavior to exist in the safety and covenant of marriage and nowhere else. Our purity is simply our willingness to wait for marriage before engaging in sexual intimacy and to adhere to God's standard of how he created romantic human relationships to function in order that we might find joy and peace in the midst of it.

Why do I tell you this story? Is it even meaningful to this chapter and the ground I hope to cover with you? I share this with you so that you will know that I have messed up in my past; I know how hard this area is. I have learned and changed. Unfortunately, I have too often had to learn from mistakes I've made rather than trusting others' advice. Can you relate? There might be some of you reading these words right now with a spotless past in the area of purity, and I celebrate with you in that. I commend you for holding strong in the face of temptation and impurity. For others, maybe you've crossed a line or two but reeled it back in quickly. Then there are those of you who have been like me: you've crossed more than one or two lines. You've made some mistakes; and it's played a part in shaping you and forming you. I want you to know that wherever you find yourself right now, from the poster child for purity to the one who draws new lines just to cross them, I see you.

Where Are You Going?

Something I really enjoy is driving and seeing new places. Sometimes I will drive around town or take the longer route home just to see the sights. I don't use a GPS, because it's all from memory. However, there are other times where I'll be taking an extended drive, and I need to know before I ever leave how I am going to get there. I pull out my phone, open the GPS, and put in my destination to map the journey. As I go, it's a constant process of turning and merging, speeding up and slowing down, and doing what must be done at the right time in the right way to safely arrive at my destination.

In your relationship, it's important that you recall and remember your destination. For most of us, that destination is marriage. We're hoping to find the right partner and make a good life together. To get there, there are things that must be done and handled correctly. The one that seems to corrupt relationships the most often is purity. All it takes is one wrong road or one missed turn to take you to a different place. If you're hoping to move closer to marriage with your significant other, and if you and your partner are living in purity, read this for encouragement. If you and your partner are at odds with purity, then read this for a new perspective.

It's very important to understand that purity doesn't only have to do with singleness, dating, and engagement. It's important for marriage as well. So what does purity really consist of? Paul had some strong words regarding this in his letter to the church of Colossae: "Put to death, therefore, whatever belongs to your earthly nature: sexual immorality, impurity, lust, evil desires and greed, which is idolatry" (Colossians 3:5).

For some, the pursuit of purity might simply mean not crossing physical boundaries; for others, it could mean setting parameters in your relationship that you will not spend time with someone of the opposite gender alone without others around. The physical marker of purity does change based on the season of life in which you find yourself, and the status of your relationship. However, the lifelong pursuit of purity is to do whatever needs to be done in your unique relationship in order to honor God above everything else. This alone is the highest goal. For some, this will look a bit stricter than others. For example, before we were married I put apps and blocking filters on my devices to not allow any access to pornography, and Chelsea and I spent most of our time together in public spaces. Now, in marriage, we still use protective apps and hold the rule I mentioned earlier that we do not spend time with someone of the opposite gender alone, but of course we do not adhere to a previous boundary of spending most of our time in public. These practices might not be the ones you choose for yourselves, but the point is to remember that how you protect your purity will change based on the season of life you and your significant other are in. The common belief seems to be that if we can just get to the wedding, then all our temptation will go by the wayside and we will never feel destructive sexual desires or struggle with porn addiction again. Unfortunately, it's just not that way. Purity matters just as much (if not more) in marriage than in dating. Pursue purity now in dating and engagement so that you might find yourself well-practiced in marriage. A friend told me this years ago, and it has stuck with me: "The enemy will do all he can to get the two of you in bed before marriage. Then, he will do all he can to keep you out of bed once you are married."

What the Data Says

I hope it's abundantly clear that I care about relationships functioning within God's best plans for them. And here's what some objective research has to say on the subject.

Dr. Andrew Magers of The Well Clinic evaluated several different studies on the subject of premarital sex and its effects on physiology and psychology. He says, "Researchers found that those who wait to have sex until marriage, compared to those who don't, report significantly higher relationship satisfaction (20%), better communication patterns (12%), less consideration of divorce (22%), and better sexual quality (15%)."[2]

Data from the National Survey of Family Growth indicate that "women who are sexually active prior to marriage faced considerably higher risk of marital disruption than women who were virgin brides." These scholars explain that even when controlling for various differentials between virginal and nonvirginal groups—such as socioeconomics, family background as well as attitudinal and value differences—"Non-virgins still face a much higher risk of divorce than virgins."[3]

If you are not a virgin, this is not intended to cast shame on you. I wasn't a virgin when I got married, and the regret I carried into our marriage because of it was immense. However, if that is you, I invite you to walk into a new way of doing relationships, and also allow your past to be healed and forgiven by God so that you can walk in power and holiness in the days ahead.

Additionally, living together prior to marriage, more commonly known as "cohabiting" has been shown to have considerably negative effects on the longevity and quality of relationships. Researchers at the Institute for Family Studies found that "living together before marriage is associated with lower odds of divorce in the first year of marriage, but increases the odds of divorce in all other years tested, and this finding holds across decades of data."[4]

If the data shows that sexual involvement prior to marriage, along with cohabiting, drives down levels of relational happiness and quality, then wouldn't we be better off waiting until marriage to experience these things? I realize some of you may be dating someone who is unwilling to budge in this area. You might consider this to be a telling sign of where and how the relationship will go in the future. If there is unwillingness to change their (or your) minds and wait on a sexual relationship for marriage, then I'd advise you to end the relationship—this is not someone you want to marry. I believe the data is simply proving what Scripture has spoken for two to three thousand years prior to these studies being done: whenever we live outside of God's design for relationship and marriage, it is only hurting us rather than helping us in the long run.

Dispelling Some Lies

But what about the common phrases our culture uses to normalize or justify these behaviors? Here are a couple of the myths I want to address:

Lie #1: "You Need to Test-Drive It before You Buy It"

"You need to test-drive it before you buy it" might be one of the most used phrases to try to justify sex before marriage. The tactic lures someone in by trying to justify the selfish behavior on the grounds of figuring out if there is physical connection and compatibility, and it is quite commonly used.

Not only is this idea wrong, but it's also selfish. I completely agree that I prefer to test drive a vehicle before I commit to purchasing it, but that sentiment regarding an automobile can't legitimately be applied to people in an attempt to justify using others to fulfill one's own sexual desires. Let me be clear—people are people; cars are cars. I like to tour a home before I buy it too. I love to walk through the rooms, ask questions about it, and have it inspected prior to purchase. Oddly enough, we don't see many people hiring inspectors to come and do a full analysis of their significant other's skin, hair, and fingernails prior to marriage, or sending them for a psychological exam with a full series of questions. That would be crazy!

God made man and woman compatible sexually—he knew exactly what he was doing. I understand that the desire for sex can be strong. We were designed to be attracted to the opposite sex, but our attraction does not justify selfishness. Whenever a phrase like this is used, it is selfish because it makes the relationship about "me" rather than "us." It takes the focus off of being a team for the glory of God and instead asks, "Will they do what I need them to do in bed to make me happy?" If you've found yourself here, there is always a chance to turn around and go in a new direction. You don't have to stay in this place. You can walk into the fullness of who God created you to be and how he designed you for relationship with him and with your partner.

Lie #2: "Porn Won't Affect My Relationship"

The idea that porn won't affect our relationships might just be one of the greatest lies of this generation. According to Covenant Eyes, a private company dedicated to stopping porn usage, "90% of teens and 96% of young adults are either encouraging, accepting, or neutral when they talk about porn with their friends."[5] This probably isn't shocking or surprising to you. However, what you might not know is that:

- **68% of divorce cases** involved one party meeting a new lover over the internet.
- **56% involved** one party having "an obsessive interest in pornographic websites."
- **70% of wives** of sex addicts could be diagnosed with PTSD.[6]

I know for many of us, porn either has been or currently is a tender place of struggle in our own lives. It definitely was for me. It might be the place where shame has crept in and told you lies about yourself, but it doesn't have to be that way any longer.

I know for myself, porn was one of those things that was always taboo to talk about, and it was fairly easy to keep hidden. So many of those I went to school with, worked with, even went to church with were dealing with the same struggles, but nobody talked about it because we didn't want to seem messed up. If you are reading this book, you probably don't need much convincing of the facts surrounding porn usage. It's found to decrease sexual satisfaction in marriage, fuel sex trafficking, increase mental illnesses, promote sexual violence, and the list could go on and on, but I'm not necessarily here to discuss those things (although they are worthy of discussion). I want to talk about the lie that porn, if being consumed in a relationship, will not affect that relationship.

In recent studies, researchers found that "*partners* of porn consumers also report negative effects, such as lower self-esteem, worse relationship quality, and less sexual satisfaction."[7] Research also suggests that porn consumption can undermine trust in a relationship and fuel couple conflict.[8] Obviously, relationship problems like these are not new and are not solely caused by porn. Yet research shows that porn can play a substantial role in fueling these issues—and that's not something that should be ignored."[9] So while you might not think that pornography has the capacity to do much harm to your relationship, the research would say something different. We always underestimate how our sin will hurt others—once again, I unfortunately speak from experience. Porn can and will hurt you and your relationship. The momentary gratification comes at a great cost, and the damage dealt to your own heart overflows into your relationship. Don't give it a place in your life; fight back and fight for purity.

If you yourself have struggled with porn usage or you're currently with someone who does, there are a couple of excellent resources I trust and believe in to help you get a foothold and further your understanding of porn use and its effects on our world and culture today. They are Covenant Eyes and Fight the New Drug. I would highly encourage you to take some time to investigate these resources for yourself, your partner, or even a friend who needs freedom.

A New Way of Thinking

So where do we go from here? I believe that freedom in purity and in life comes by way of the Word of God. Jesus said in John 8:32, "You will know the truth, and the truth will set you free." Let me ask you right now: Is purity an area where you need to find freedom? I love what Jesus goes on to say two verses later, right after some Jewish followers claimed that they had never been slaves to anyone, so why would they need freedom? Jesus replied, "Very truly I tell you, everyone who sins is a slave to sin" (verse 34). We are all sinners, every single one of us (Romans 3:23), and we all need the freedom that only Jesus can give. I can point you to resources, guides, and websites, but if I don't point you to the King, the Prince of Peace, the very one who saved me and gave me a fresh start and a new life, then this book wouldn't be worth the paper it's printed on.

Now, back to John 8:32 for a moment. I believe that Jesus is both making an identity claim and asserting a promise here. Jesus seems to be saying that when they recognize Jesus for who he actually is, they will see that he is the truth of God incarnate. And he, being the truth in bodily form, will indeed set them free (forgiveness) from the very thing he said was holding them captive (sin). So Jesus is truth, and he will set free those who know him by forgiving them of their sin.

What does this have to do with purity? We need to recognize that purity doesn't come by way of trying harder or keeping more rules and regulations. Instead, purity begins in the heart. But how can that be if our hearts are stricken with this disease called sin (Jeremiah 17:9)? If purity begins in our hearts, and our hearts are wicked because of sin, then we need new hearts! The prophet Ezekiel wrote these words that he heard directly from God: "I will give you a new heart and put a new spirit in you; I will remove from you your heart of stone and give you a heart of flesh" (Ezekiel 36:26). The context of this verse and chapter is that God was promising to heal his people, restore them, save them, free them, and establish them once again.

When you receive Christ by faith, you have received a new heart. He has made you a new creation (2 Corinthians 5:17). You still have the ability to walk in sin as a believer, but it is by your own choice. You have power over it and don't have to submit to it.

There is one verse in the Bible that I wish I would've meditated on earlier in life. I find myself thinking about it more now than I ever have, and I think it will always be one that cuts through the noise and reminds me of God's intention for my life. Maybe you need it today or tomorrow, or every day like I do. In Psalm 24:3–4 King David wrote these words, which have been and will continue to be my prayer: "Who may ascend the mountain of the LORD? Who may stand in his holy place? The one who has clean hands and a pure heart, who does not trust in an idol or swear by a false god." Clean hands and a pure heart. It is the sin in the human heart that causes the wickedness of human hands. Jesus is ready to forgive your sin and heal your heart. Will you let him?

What If I Mess Up?

We know we want to pursue a life of purity before and after marriage, but now the inevitable question looms large: What if I mess up again? My mentor and friend Clayton instilled a saying in my heart and mind some years ago that I have never forgotten: "When you mess up, fess up." The best thing you can do on the other side of messing up or falling flat on your face is exactly as follows.

1. Confess to an older trusted adviser (mentor, pastor, trusted leader of the same sex if possible).
2. Acknowledge to your partner that what you (or both of you) did was wrong and that repentance is needed.
3. Create a boundary to keep it from happening again. Have conversations about it often to ensure that it doesn't remain a problem.
4. Seek to honor God and find healing through the prayer of others (James 5:16).

If you happen to make a mistake (you will), whether in the context of singleness, dating, engagement, or even marriage, don't allow it to derail you. I'm not going to cancel my annual vacation trip that I have saved up for, invested in, planned, and anticipated just because I hit a pothole and got a flat tire on the way to the airport. A mess-up or mistake might cause a minor delay or inconvenience, but it doesn't mean we need to cancel the trip. Jump right back on course where you left off, own your mistake, and then work through it as best you can. However, don't let the wiggle room of mistakes allow you to feel as though you have the liberty to sin—considerable repercussions and correction come along with these mistakes. There comes a point when a lack of maturity must be recognized and addressed so that you and your partner don't continue hurting each other. This will mean committing to surrounding yourselves with the right people, working hard, having healthy conversations, spending time in public, and pursuing the heart of God together. You can do it!

Should I Go Forward?

So what do you think? Where have you been in your relationship as it pertains to purity? What do you think is the right move or the smart call at this point in time? Do you believe you have honored one another but have just made a mistake here and there? Has it been a constant cycle of messing up then trying to do better until you mess up again? Has there been any regard for the potential damage being done? Have any secrets been kept hidden so that nobody will get upset?

This is an opportunity to be brutally honest and transparent with yourself about where your relationship stands. I know it might scare you to think about a life without your partner, but what should scare you more is living a life together while serious issues go unresolved. Take this time to think carefully and discuss honestly, remembering that deciding to go forward with marriage is no small choice to make.

REFLECTION QUESTIONS

Here are some questions to help you reflect.

- Does my significant other love Jesus?
- Do we honor one another with our bodies?
- Would we be comfortable doing around others what we do in private?
- Do we care what God asks of us in regard to purity?

- Do I have any hidden issues that I should talk to a trusted adviser about?
- Am I just committed to the relationship because of how physically involved we are?

A Few Words from Chelsea

Nick and I honestly feel this chapter alone could be a whole book. There is so much to say! But I want to mention something to look out for in yourself or in your partner. Living in a society that normalizes heavy social media use can be grounds for you to set up some boundaries here as well. The images our eyes see lead to thoughts we have, and our thoughts could potentially lead to action. So it's wise to guard what your eyes see on these apps. Some apps don't filter or monitor explicit content. Sometimes the content might not even be explicit, but it causes jealousy or impure thoughts that could lead to sin. I deleted Twitter because of this! Trust me, your life will mature even more when you recognize what is unhealthy and how to guard yourself and your relationship. This doesn't stop after marriage either. Both my husband and I ask each other regularly what we are seeing on our phones and hold each other accountable.

Our hearts are not to condemn or shame anyone. We know what it's like to live a life according to what we think is best for ourselves, but we've learned that God desires for our intimacy to be beautiful and whole, even if our past may include sexual shame or abuse. I am so sorry if that is part of your story. Hope and healing are available to you, and I pray you'll get professional help if you haven't already. We are so thankful for God's grace and protection over both us and you as we lean into wisdom for guarding the beauty of sexual intimacy.

#7 CAN YOU ENJOY A LIFE TOGETHER?

Chelsea

I could feel the whirl of excitement in the air as I walked through Forest Park, Missouri, on a calm and unseasonably warm winter day. Around me were people out enjoying the weather, flying kites, and running. A beautiful grassy hillside rose next to a body of water where geese and couples in paddle boats were gliding through the water. I thought of how perfect the day had been so far. Nick (who was just my friend a few weeks prior) had flown all the way to Illinois where I lived to spend a few days with me. He hadn't asked me to be his girlfriend yet, but I could sense that he was going to. We had already been through a lot together, even before this trip. Weeks before, I'd been struggling to sleep consistently and spent hours crying in my room, and I thought those things were normal at the time. Fast-forward a month and I was in recovery after being in the psych unit of the hospital for mental illness. Nick called me every day to see how I was doing in the hospital and to ask how he could be praying for me. A lot of my friends at the time were confused and didn't know what to say or do through such a tough time. Nick seemed to know all the right questions to ask and even consistently sent letters during my stay there. We had endless FaceTime calls getting to know each other, and my feelings for him were growing stronger as time went on.

So before we even started dating, whenever Nick would tell me he loved me, it didn't seem out of the ordinary. We had started as loving, caring friends, so it wasn't necessarily romantic. From the start, we both found each other attractive, but Nick agreed when we first met that he wouldn't try to date me as I was healing from a previous relationship and I had asked that he respect that decision.

Nonetheless, we couldn't help but develop feelings for each other, and I had never experienced a relationship as healthy as this one.

The sun was setting in Forest Park, while we were on our first "official" date. I told Nick I loved him back as we sat next to the water with our feet dangling over the ledge. He leaned in slowly, and we kissed for the first time. I could have jumped up and down from how energized I felt (I was majorly crushin'). I love that my first memories of my now husband are of slow and thoughtful moments of pursuit. Not only did Nick tell me frequently his intentions in our dating relationship, but he showed me that he respected and cherished me too. Because our first year of being together was long distance, we wanted to create memories that were unique like our date in the park. I smile every time I recall how God was so intentional with our relationship from the start.

Years into our relationship, I will admit that the butterflies I felt in the beginning are not there in the way they were originally. But I don't think this is a bad thing! Ask any older couple that has been together for years, and they will tell you that their love may look different than it did in the beginning, but it has grown, becoming stronger and more certain through trials and experience. Just because marriage will look different as the years go by doesn't mean you can't enjoy each other in every season. There is so much joy in growing together and in watching your partner grow, even if their growth looks different from yours. We shouldn't be scared or intimidated by the growth we see, but rather trust that God will keep us growing together as well. The beautiful thing about growing with the one you love is seeing the same person renewed over and over as they change.

As we ask the question, Is the person I'm with the right one as my life partner?, it's important to consider whether they care about your likes and interests! Do they want to invest their time and energy into things you care about? Early on in dating, I remember wanting to do anything and everything with Nick. If he was there, I was going to have fun and enjoy my time. If he wanted to stare at a wall for hours, I would be happy to join him in that (well, not really, but you get my point).

As time went on, we both grew separately and together in the things we enjoyed. We had our separate passions that we pursued individually, and those were only growing. I discovered that I love talking with friends any chance I get (like going to coffee shops), and Nick started to get more and more into his love of sports cars. We still enjoyed spending time with each other, but we also loved doing our own thing. It wasn't until a recent conversation that we realized we weren't putting much effort into doing activities that involved each other's passions and likes. We had each become a little selfish in how we liked to spend our time—holding firm to our individual passions while the other person protected theirs. We forgot what the point was—to enjoy time together no matter what we did! Since this talk, we have intentionally tried to do things that we enjoy *together*, such as watching a good movie even if one or both of us might prefer a different genre, or taking turns choosing the restaurant or take-out place. We even ask each other on date night about our interests and what has been intriguing us lately in our alone time. It looks different each and every time we hang out. In your relationship, it is so important to express what you enjoy individually while continuing to have the goal of being together and sharing life together. That doesn't mean you quit doing anything on your own—just that you balance your personal pursuits with intentional quality time together.

> The beautiful thing about growing with the one you love is seeing the same person renewed over and over as they change.

My personality makes it easy for me to take a back seat around others who are more vocal and stronger in their opinions (there is nothing wrong with having a strong personality!), but I've learned that it benefits my husband when I choose to share my opinion and not shy away because I'm afraid of disagreement.

To help you acknowledge and accept your differences in personal preference (or maybe your similarities!), I've provided a chart for you to fill out. Truly lean in as you fill out this list, listening to each other's interests and remembering that the goal of this exercise is to *be* with one another. Observe how your significant other responds to the things you list!

	Her Thoughts	His Thoughts
Favorite way to spend a Friday night		
Favorite type of food		
You're bored— what do you do?		
Who do you look up to?		
What do you love to talk about?		

A Heart of Celebration

I remember the first time I decided to surprise Nick with something out of the ordinary for his birthday. We were newly dating at this point, and I decided to give his apartment a makeover. He moved into his new place not too long before I decided to do this for him, so he was sleeping on an air mattress. I ended up getting a mattress and patio furniture for him, and I redid his living room. I was so pumped to reveal all the work I put into making his day special, and when I showed it to him, he was shocked. We still look back to this day as a special time in our relationship because I'm pretty sure he started shopping for a ring around this time! Coincidence? Now, I'm not implying you go deck out your person's home, but celebrating one another has been a key part of our relationship. If we can find a reason to celebrate, we do!

Does the person you're with have a heart to celebrate you and your wins? What about your wins as a couple? Celebrating together puts into perspective what is important and what is not. I've created a list of ideas for you to glean from—feel free to make it your own!

Ways to Celebrate

- Write an annual letter to each other for Christmas, New Year's, the day you met or started dating, or birthdays.
- Come up with a tradition you can celebrate each year and look back on in future years.
- Create an anniversary scrapbook that you add to over time.
- Whenever a special moment comes up, like a job promotion, go out to dinner or on a special outing to celebrate!
- Write out lists affirming the qualities and traits you appreciate in one another.

I love to follow older couples online who have been married for decades. They truly know how to celebrate one another. One of the couples I follow recently went on a trip to Europe for an entire month. They saved up for years to celebrate a huge milestone of being together for thirty years. I'm reminded of all the marriage events I've been to and how the oldest couple in the room is typically applauded for their faithfulness in enduring so many seasons together. That is my goal with my husband. I know we have a long way to go, but what an incredible story of God's grace to have been in a marriage for fifty-plus years. As you think about your future, how do you view the person you are dating? Do you see them as someone you'll gaze at across the dinner table one day when you're both old and gray?

Expectations for Sex

Before I got married, I ran to all the premarital advice books and went straight to the section on sex. Just me? It's valid to be excited about intimacy with the one you love dearly, if you do end up married! God wired us for intimacy, and sex is a beautiful gift! I think one of the reasons God designed sex the way he did is because we all long to be known and seen as cherished, valuable, and desirable. But physical intimacy isn't all that marriage is built upon. Intimacy is found in the understanding of one another, the spiritual foundation your relationship is established upon, your emotional bond, your intellectual connection, and most importantly, the kingdom purpose you have together. There is so much more to marriage than just sex!

I walked into marriage without a sexual past. I had kissed other guys I had dated but didn't have sex until my wedding night. I will say that the temptation beforehand was very strong. It's tough to hold out on a good thing that God designed with the one you love so much. But I do see now why sex is something the Lord desires to be within the confines of marriage. Nick had a sexual past before we got married, which was a bit tough to work through at first. I would self-consciously compare myself to the girls he had been with in the past, but he always reassured me in those moments and reminded me that he desired a different, and better, future with me.

No matter your past in this area, it's easy to have expectations of how intimacy will play out in your future marriage. Some mentors of ours painted intimacy in a way that has stuck with me: Imagine a fire outside on a cold winter day. The fire is blazing and hot and provides warmth. But if that fire gets outside of the parameters that keeps it confined, it is no longer simply a warm fire. It starts to consume and destroy everything outside of the barriers. It is no longer an enjoyable and beautiful thing. It is destructive and dangerous. I love to think of this picture as how sex works inside marriage and outside marriage. There are boundaries in our sex lives in marriage and boundaries in dating relationships for a good reason. They are for our protection and good. Discussing your expectations for sex and intimacy is crucial before taking your relationship forward in this area. It is not healthy to operate under assumptions about each other's past or what your intimacy will look like in marriage.

Before I got married, I had the view that sex was the most glorious thing in the world and something I was going to want to do all the time. (I obviously had no idea what to expect.) In the weeks leading up to when Nick and I said "I do," we had lots of conversations around sex and our expectations and thoughts about it all. We broke down our past hurts and our hopes for making this part of our marriage pure and special.

I can confirm after years of a physical relationship with my husband that it is wonderful, but I also had deep relational **Boundaries are for our protection and good.** needs I was trying to meet within marriage that could not be fulfilled by sex. These needs actually couldn't be filled by my husband at all! Only Christ can give me the fulfillment I need in terms of love, contentment, and security. Yes, Nick can provide these, but not in the way Jesus can.

If I could encourage anything in this area, I would press you and your significant other to have some serious conversations about sex. Open up about expectations and the boundaries you'd like to set or reinforce. Here is a list of conversation starters that might help!

REFLECTION QUESTIONS

- How are we going to have a pure sexual relationship leading up to marriage?
- What was your past like with those you dated previously?
- What are your future expectations of sex in marriage?
- Are there any fears you have surrounding intimacy?

During these talks, you may find out that there is a healthy amount of understanding, or you may need to have more talks like these to see if your expectations are truly good and realistic. If you feel unsettled or pressured or sense a lack of respect, this is a red flag. Lean into that feeling and ask the Lord to show you the way out if that is the case. I pray these talks are meaningful and encouraging to you.

Break Up the Routine

When Nick and I had our first child, we found out just how quickly life can feel like a loop of the same responsibilities and routines over and over. As much as the structure is valuable and important, we realized how much our marriage thrives when we get away for a few days or invite a babysitter over so we can have a few hours to ourselves.

What do date nights look like for you? Is the person you are dating willing to drop their plans for you and spend time with you? What are their priorities?

Having a day of the week to look forward to as you go through your job, chores, and obligations makes the week more fun and exciting as you anticipate a new experience or some downtime together. It may not be in the budget for every couple to explore a new restaurant weekly, but there is something you can do to enjoy time together on a regular basis. To give you a few ideas for quality time and date nights, here's a mini list!

- Explore something new in the town where you live—maybe a downtown walk, a bookstore, a hiking trail, even a new ice cream place. Just try something new together!
- Go for a walk in the park and grab a meal to eat outside.
- Play twenty questions in your own living room.
- Visit a local museum.
- Go on a coffee shop tour.
- Take out the board games and play.
- Make a new meal from scratch together.
- Go on a night run to both of your favorite fast-food places.
- Watch a show together that you both watched as kids, or share a show you watched as a kid that is new to the other.
- Watch a comedy movie together.
- Do a seasonal activity (for example, apple picking, ice skating, etc.).

It doesn't really matter what you do. What matters is that you're carving out time that you both agree to enjoy together!

As They Change

After my mental illness episode early in my relationship with Nick, I realized that he had known a version of me that was not the "normal" Chelsea. However, the core of who I was stayed the same. Thankfully, Nick embraced the changes I went through and continues to do so. I have seen him change over time as well, as he has shifted jobs, become a dad, gone through loss, and embraced new moves as a family. Each time something forces us to adapt to our new surroundings and challenges, it is uncomfortable at first—there have even been arguments and downright ugliness in the process. But as we choose to stick together through those times and ask the Lord what he is trying to change in our hearts—he always reveals it!

The person you choose to marry will likely go through some shifts in their heart and may not be the exact same today as they will be twenty years from now. We are constantly learning, changing, evolving, and it's a wonderful thing!

REFLECTION QUESTIONS

- Has your significant other been open to you changing during the time of your relationship? How do they respond when you don't do what they expect?
- Have you seen your significant other make changes for the better for themselves? What have those looked like?
- What is their mindset on change? Does it scare them? Do they welcome it? Do you?

Fit for Each Other

Then the LORD God said, "It is not good that the man should be alone; I will make him a helper fit for him." Now out of the ground the LORD God had formed every beast of the field and every bird of the heavens and brought them to the man to see what he would call them. And whatever the man called every living creature, that was its name. The man gave names to all livestock and to the birds of the heavens and to every beast of the field. But for Adam there was not found a helper fit for him. So the LORD God caused a deep sleep to fall upon the man, and while he slept took one of his ribs and closed up its place with flesh. And the rib that the LORD God had taken from the man he made into a woman and brought her to the man. (Genesis 2:18–22 ESV)

I find it so beautifully intentional of God to design us to be wired for one another. To help each other through life, man and woman were created. Two reflections of God's image in over 7 billion ways all over the world. All of us look, speak, and live differently. No two people are the same—yet he calls us to partner with him in our marriages. Isn't that crazy amazing?

Several of the guys I dated before Nick progressively seemed more serious and began to look more like "marriage material" as I got older. I thought the man I dated before Nick would be my husband at some point, but I knew in my spirit, after conversations with friends and family, that we just were not "fit" for each other. Now, I'm not implying that all the stars must align and a sign from the clouds has to shine down telling you that you and the person you're dating are perfect for one another. But for me, I knew that Nick and I were fit for each other. There was a feeling I couldn't shake and a call from God early in our relationship that made sense to me and to him. It carried us through tough seasons when we thought we might break up and kept us secure through even our long-distance season.

Of course, we have rough edges, and there will be rough seasons when you will feel like strangers, but there should be an initial connection of enjoyment in one another and a conviction in knowing you are marrying rightly. A few questions I would challenge you to sit with are: Is this someone who fits you, someone you can enjoy and celebrate even as they grow and change? And do you and they have the character necessary to continue pursuing enjoyment and friendship together through the shifting seasons?

A Few Words from Nick

Fun and enjoyment are some of the things we tend to forget about or move on from the older we get, aren't they? We get bogged down by the pressures of life—jobs, bills, schedules, and the next obligation on our calendar. While some seasons of life will inevitably be more difficult or strenuous, try to make it a priority to have fun. This will probably look different for you than it will for us, but it is crucial. When we stop having fun or making opportunities for fun, we're missing out on a beautiful gift! I believe there are many reasons God refers to us as little children in the Bible, one of them being that we must rely on God as a little child relies on his parent with total trust, just believing that his parent will be there no matter what. I also like to believe God refers to us in this way because kids love to have fun. When we're living our lives in the context of God's design for our relationships, we open ourselves up to living a life of fun with our spouse.

Not every moment or season of life will be one of great enjoyment. There will certainly be hard days, weeks, and months, but when we commit to working through those things together and enjoying the life we get to live, times of pleasure and fun help put things into perspective. Remember that God created relationships as a beautiful expression of his covenant with the church, and that is truly something to celebrate and enjoy to the fullest extent.

#8 HOW DO YOU HANDLE SECRETS?

Nick

It was November 2017, and Chelsea and I had been dating for about eight months. I had flown up to St. Louis to be with her and her family for about a week while we were still in a long-distance relationship. In the days leading up to the trip, a girl I used to date had reached out to me to check in and see how I was doing. I told her I'd been well, and naturally I asked how she had been. Things soon got pretty weird—she began telling me how hard things had been since our relationship ended and how she'd like to sit down over lunch and discuss things further. I had moved on, and she knew I was dating Chelsea.

The whole interaction from our texts to our phone calls was really strange, and it seemed she was trying to convince me to end my current relationship with Chelsea to get back together again. I chose not to tell Chelsea as I thought it was unnecessary and wouldn't help anything. While we were at dinner, my phone lit up with a text from my ex-girlfriend saying, "Hope to see you soon." Chelsea saw it, and the next thirty minutes were really tense. I had to explain everything, and she really struggled for a few weeks, wondering if I was keeping anything else from her, if I was going to break up with her for my ex, and so many other things. Our relationship suffered for the next month, and because I hadn't told her sooner, I didn't know if we were going to make it. Through a lot of conversations and honesty, we did. I know now that if I'd just told her what was really going on from the beginning, things would have been much easier to work through. Secrets are never worth keeping.

I guess it's clear from this opening story that I have been in a place where I had secrets. I had many of them, some of them minor and some of them quite weighty. If that is you, please know that I understand exactly how that feels. You probably feel as though it's simply easier to keep those things to yourself rather than air them out for others to see. That is a great plan in theory; it allows you to keep what you hope to hide to yourself and not "burden" others with those things. That's what the enemy has told you, isn't it? What would others think of you if they knew what you had done? I'll tell you: they are going to think you are just like them, because you are. Let me free you up a bit here. Every single person has, or has had at a point in time, some things they never wanted others to find out about. I am no exception, and I doubt you are either.

I saw a video some years ago that has stayed with me. A professor was in his classroom lecturing his students, using a glass of water as his illustration. He was questioning his students about how hard it would be to hold up a glass of water for one minute. The class muttered for a short moment until it was evident that it would not be very hard to hold up a glass of water for one minute. The professor then asked what would happen if he held it up for one hour. He shared that it was likely his arm would go numb. Then he took it a step further and asked what would happen if he held the glass of water all day, straight out in front of him. He said it would be impossible, as fatigue would set in and his muscles would give out. So why couldn't he hold up the glass all day? It was not that the weight of the glass had changed, but rather how long he had to hold it.

Many of us walk through our lives with the incredible burden of trying to carry these secrets all day every day. How about taking a moment to set down the cup? Expose that which has long been hidden and bring it to light to find the freedom that is available for you today. It changed everything for me.

The Power of Confession

Chelsea and I were meeting with a couple from our church for premarital counseling. In the middle of one of our discussions, I felt a deep conviction come over me, and a sudden burst of anxiety shot through my body even just thinking about sharing a deep and dark secret I'd been wrestling with. I mustered up the courage, knowing this was a safe and wise space to share, and I admitted it. I'd been struggling with pornography while I was dating Chelsea. The words that followed from the husband were some of the most comforting words I think I've ever heard. He looked at me in the middle of sharing something so deeply personal and said, "I'm proud of you for being willing to confess. What you are doing is not okay, but you are not alone and we want to help."

That was exactly what I needed to hear and what is available to you as well. What you did might not be okay, but you are not alone. You are not any less loved by God or by others, and I hope this chapter will help you walk the road to freedom.

There are many different kinds of secrets we carry, aren't there? For some of us it's a lot of dysfunction in our family, or poor management of our finances that has gotten us into a major hole financially. For others it could be a sexual history, poor decisions you made, something that someone else did to you, or even a certain health challenge—physical, mental, or emotional. Many of the secrets we harbor aren't even sinful; they might just be insecurities or shame about some component of our life that we don't want others to know about. That is completely understandable, and it is human nature to want to preserve our reputation by being selective about what we do and do not share. However, if we don't change our view on keeping secrets and allow people into these areas of our lives, we will miss out on much of the healing that God wants for us, as well as the trust of the person we're in a relationship with.

I'm sure you've noticed some of the things going on right now within our generation. Many young people don't have a complete sense of who they are. We do a lot of things to try to make ourselves appear better or more put together. We can begin lying to others about struggles we do or do not face, and then we begin believing the lies we are telling. We can create a false sense of who we actually are and begin losing touch with our true self as a result. The fastest way to combat this is by confessing, being open and honest about our failures and struggles and sharing our desire to turn things around. I can speak about the power of confession with such confidence because this was me. I was in my late teens, in a heaping mess of lying to myself about who I really was, and in doing so, I lost my sense of self. I had covered up my true self mostly so that other people would like me and think more highly of me and so that my friends would think I was good enough to hang out with them.

What I discovered was that I was deeply and bitterly insecure. We often treat insecurity like the enemy to be avoided at all costs. But every single one of us, myself included, either has been or currently is insecure about something in our life. For me, acknowledging this insecurity was truly a major sigh of relief. I had grown desperately sick of trying to perform and impress others around me, and to finally have someone call out the heart issue of insecurity meant someone cared enough about me to notice and help me start to treat it. You cannot hope to improve your situation—along with your life and relationships—until you have come to a point of complete honesty with yourself and others.

What God Says

In the Bible, one of the well-known writers of the New Testament was named Paul. Here was a man with a wild story. He was a Jewish scholar and leader who was once known for persecuting the early Christian church and murdering Christians in the process. Long story short—God shows himself to Paul one day, and everything about Paul is changed in a single moment. He finally sees that Jesus is actually the Son of God, the Lord and Savior of humanity. But Paul had a major dilemma on his hands. He was now part of the very group that he had just been persecuting. I wonder what happened when he showed up and told them for the first time that he was a follower of Jesus. I'd have to bet that conversation was a tad bit awkward.

Paul would go on to write these words in 2 Corinthians 12:9 that I think hold profound power for each of us. "But [God] said to me, 'My grace is sufficient for you, for my power is made perfect in weakness.' Therefore I will boast all the more gladly about my weaknesses, so that Christ's power may rest on me." That's a great verse, but what does it have to do with secrets? I know I viewed the secrets in my life as personal places of weakness. I felt inferior and less than because of the things in my past, the things I'd tried really hard to keep covered up so that nobody would know the real me, mired in mistakes and regrets. It's usually these places in our lives where God can do the deepest work for our own good and for others to see as a symbol of hope—hope that God can redeem even the messiest parts of our stories. That was certainly the case for Paul, and for myself too. In short, it is important for you to remember that everyone has a past, and everyone has made mistakes. You will find power over these things in your life when they are brought to light and when you allow God to heal them and then redeem and use them for his glory and the good of others. Your story is nothing to be afraid of, but it's most powerful when we are sincere about what we have really experienced and gone through.

It's Time to Uncover the Truth

After a secret is revealed to someone, they'll often say something like, "You're just now telling me?" or, "Why didn't you tell me sooner?" The more time that goes by as we hold on to our secrets, the more we end up harming our significant other and our relationship by choosing not to trust them. Once a secret is revealed, the person inevitably wonders why we didn't tell them sooner. They feel hurt and betrayed, not understanding why we didn't trust them. Imagine yourself in the other person's shoes for a moment. You've been dating for quite some time, they've told you they love you and trust you, yet they choose to withhold from you decisions they have made or are currently making, maybe things that would hurt you deeply if you found out. Would you feel trusted or loved if you knew that was the case? Probably not. But what if instead of hiding their secret, they chose to humble themselves—no matter how many times it has happened before—go directly to you, admit their wrongdoing, their would-be secret, and ask you for forgiveness? You'd maybe feel hurt, and their confession might cause a rift for a moment, but you'd know you could trust them because they chose to expose what was really going on rather than keep it to themselves.

For a long time I thought I was helping by not sharing with Chelsea some bad decisions I'd made in the past that were still affecting my life, and consequently hers. I figured if I just breezed over them, chose to "start new" and move on from where I was, there was no need to look back in the past, right? I grew up in a farming and construction family, working primarily in the area of flooring. I learned one thing early on that I remember to this day. You cannot build or put a new floor on a cracked or broken foundation. Don't ask me why—just believe me when I tell you that it cannot be done if you want a quality floor. In the same way, you cannot possibly hope to have a successful relationship or marriage if it is sitting on a cracked or broken foundation of secrets and covering up the truth.

Last Time I Opened Up, I Got Hurt

This is where things get a bit tricky. You may be reading this and thinking about the time you chose to open up and trust someone else with a secret, only for them to share your secret with other people you had no intention of sharing with. You felt hurt, betrayed, and probably angry. I don't blame you at all; it's only natural that you felt betrayed. Someone took advantage of you whether they intended to or not. That is not okay. And now you sit here finding it difficult to trust at all. Here's the truth, though. Choosing not to open up about the difficult secrets you are carrying will end up hurting you far more in the long run than that person who betrayed you ever did.

A few years ago in college, I felt like I was alone, hurting, full of grief, and just weary. Not the kind of weary where you're physically tired so you get a good night's sleep and wake up feeling better. More than that, I felt weary in my soul. I was tired of hiding and hurting in this secret pit of sin. I was tired of making sure I presented a certain image to everyone, acting like I had it all together when I really didn't. Tired. One afternoon during that season of life, when I was in between classes and walking to a different building, my phone rang. It was one of my mentors I hadn't talked to in a few months. He was just calling to check in on me and ask how I was doing. I sat and talked with him for a few minutes. I told him I was doing fine and that things were going pretty well. Apparently I'm a terrible liar, because based on my tone he said, "Really? You don't sound like you're doing fine. You can be real with me, man." I was nervous. I didn't want people to find out what was really going on in my life. What if he went and told everyone? What if he betrayed my trust? As these thoughts were swirling through my mind, I walked out to the edge of the parking lot where nobody was and cried on the phone for fifteen minutes with him. I don't remember much of anything he told me; I just remember that I could open up and trust him. I'm glad I did. I'm not sure if you find yourself in a place like this, where it is exceedingly hard to trust people with the reality of your life because of previous hurts or the fear of being hurt, but it doesn't have to be that way. Let me encourage you as a brother, one who has been right in the middle of a life full of mistakes, that wherever you find yourself this day, you don't have to stay there. You don't have to hold on to the past any longer. Let people in.

Wisdom and Foolishness

One of the most beautiful things about a relationship that is aiming toward marriage is the ability to be real and transparent with one another. At least, it should be that way. While it's true that there was a time when Chelsea and I didn't feel like we could tell each other everything because we didn't have complete trust in one another, the only way for us to move into having that kind of trusting relationship was to be vulnerable and open about what was actually going on in our lives and hearts. If in your current relationship you never feel like you can be vulnerable, it might not be the right relationship.

There is a line of wisdom and foolishness here, though, that you'll want to be aware of. To share things that are too personal with someone you just met or someone you're not sure you'd marry probably isn't wise. However, if the man or woman you are dating is someone you can imagine yourself marrying, but you're choosing to withhold because you're uncomfortable or afraid, and you choose to end the relationship based on those feelings, then that could be foolish. For us, Chelsea was hurt more because I took so long to share these things with her than by the actual things I finally chose to share. There has to be a balance: don't be so quick to share with someone that you don't have a basis of trust established, but don't wait until you're talking about or thinking about engagement before opening up about your past.

Usually what we think will happen in this scenario is different from what actually happens. We think we'll sit them down and tell them we have some things we need to get off our chest, and they will just sit there and listen. However, what usually happens is a conversation that is beneficial for both sides. In light of this, it's a great opportunity to ask your significant other about their past or maybe some of the difficult things that haven't yet been discussed. This conversation doesn't have to be weird or awkward but can be a door of liberation that the two of you walk through together, finding freedom to move forward in strength.

I love what Solomon wrote in Proverbs 28:13: "Whoever conceals his transgressions will not prosper, but he who confesses and forsakes them will obtain mercy" (ESV). It's clear that Solomon is primarily talking about obtaining mercy from God here, but I think it happens more often than not in human relationships as well. Don't be anxious, but view a conversation about hidden things in your past as an opportunity to dive into the deep end and move one step closer to discovering if your significant other is right for you in the context of marriage and a life together.

REFLECTION QUESTIONS

The following questions are not easy to answer but are very important. Make sure they are prayed through, thought about, and carefully communicated at the right time so that you and your significant other can maintain an open and honest relationship. The exposure of secrets in our relationship took a while; we had to work through it purposefully, praying for God's guidance to help us move forward. I'd advise you to do the same thing— you'll be glad you did.

- Can you share a secret from earlier in your life that was hard to share then but might be easier now?
- Are there things we should take some time to discuss, anything we might be carrying from our past that has been hard to share that we would like to share now?
- Is there anything from your past or present that you have been keeping from me that I need to know about? I promise not to be upset or make any quick decisions here

and now, but I would like complete transparency, and I
know you would too.

- If we continue in our relationship and into marriage, can we
both work not to keep secrets from each other? How do
you think we can do that?

A Few Words from Chelsea

What if you're on the receiving end of a secret that was in the dark for
a long time, now exposed to the light for you to respond to? It can be
tempting to shut down, get defensive, and be reluctant to trust again.
I get this completely, as this has been a part of our relationship. But
what I've learned in marriage is that confession of sin or shame is part
of doing life with another believer in Jesus who needs just as much
grace as I do. I can't expect my husband to be perfect, just like he
can't expect perfection from me. So what do you do when a moment
of confession comes and everything in you wants to sit in the hurt
and say, "How could you?" I acknowledge the hurt, breathe, and ask
for patience as I process. When the anger or sadness has subsided
some, we talk through it, forgive, and plan how to help each other
move forward. I also try to put myself in Nick's shoes and figure out
why he may have chosen the route he did. And I know that whenever
I confess my sin to him, his response will be filled with grace because
we're both so aware of how much we need it.

#9 WHAT ABOUT YOUR EMOTIONAL HEALTH?

Chelsea

I can remember holding grudges toward others during certain seasons of my life. I thought if I held on to the hurt, surely the person who wronged me would apologize and realize how wrong they were. If I could go back and tell myself how unhealthy this habit was, I would, but I'm not even sure I would have been able to receive that type of advice at the time. I was emotionally unhealthy, and by that I mean my responses toward anything that would go wrong in a relationship were usually bitterness, jealousy, anger, or distrust. I found myself bossed around by the thoughts I had, and I believed I was right about my judgment of everyone. But, oh, how wrong I was.

I debated including this chapter because the topic of emotional health is often overlooked, and I wondered if maybe it wasn't important to talk about emotional health. But as I thought of my marriage now and how I've watched our emotional health improve over time, I realized this part of a relationship has the potential to improve for everyone. And when it does, it benefits both people and drastically shifts the dynamic of the relationship for the better. But to see improvement in the area of emotional health, you have to be willing to admit that you may be wrong (a lot), and that takes humility.

Emotionally healthy relationships don't lack conflict or challenging times. But emotionally healthy individuals choose to respond rationally rather than reacting emotionally in the moment. There will be times when you don't get this right (I'm the first to admit this has been me). I love what HealthyPlace says about this: "It's inevitable. People are going to disagree sometimes. People become angry, upset, irritable. In emotionally healthy relationships, people respond rather than react. They don't lose sight of their greater goal:

a loving, caring, respectful relationship with each other. As such, they focus on the issue at hand rather than on all of the personal short-comings of each other."[10]

I've had several conversations with other young married friends who have had issues in their relationships, and sometimes they have a hard time explaining what the problem is. They describe that in conversations with their spouse they notice a lack of empathy or an inability to understand, even when communication seems clear. What it sounds like is a lack of emotional intelligence. If you've never heard of emotional intelligence, it is *"the ability to understand, use, and manage your own emotions in positive ways* to relieve stress, communicate effectively, empathize with others, overcome challenges and defuse conflict."[11] I used to believe that someone was born with a certain level of emotional intelligence and it couldn't be changed. I now understand that it grows with maturity and with an awareness of our emotions and an understanding of ourselves and others. It has been amazing to see the growth in this area for me and Nick. I'd say we both lacked a bit of emotional intelligence when we first got together, but now I like to believe it will only continue to grow.

In Anger

I am more prone to anger than Nick is. It is something I've worked hard on over the years. Even in childhood, when I felt unsettled, I would allow hurt to build up inside until I couldn't take it anymore, and then the anger came spewing out all at once. Early on in our marriage, something that regularly triggered my anger was any conversation around the topic of money. Money made me angry because I saw it as a threat to our relationship.

I had a very unhealthy relationship with money growing up, and I worried that it would cause issues in my future marriage. So I thought maybe it was best to avoid the conversations all together!

I had to rid myself of this mindset as Nick and I hashed out our financial goals and worked to be on the same page. I realized the solution to my old way of thinking about finances wasn't to ignore talking about money but to talk through my fears and pain instead. Nick helped me disarm my anger and asked me questions that got to the heart of why I was believing lies about money and not trusting God's provision. We even went through a whole year of marriage counseling to address our unique pasts in relation to money, and it helped us so much.

Generally the conversations that trigger anger are not as worthy of attention as the root of the anger itself. There is always a reason a conversation might trigger feelings of discontent, frustration, or lack of control. Pulling apart the layers of *why* is worth the time. Imagine yourself entirely healed of an old pattern or mindset that felt like your default but was entirely unhealthy. Even in a small area, this could make a huge difference as you do life with the person you love!

Dr. Caroline Leaf offers some wisdom for each of us to grapple with on the subject of healthy conflict: "One of the keys to arguing well is to understand what is called your 'vulnerability cycle.' It is important to remember that the unmet emotional need behind the content of an argument is often more important than what the argument is actually about. This means understanding that whatever your vulnerability was during your childhood and based on past experiences, and how that will affect how you relate to your significant other when times get tough. For example, imagine that when your parents fought as a child, you went to your room to escape the intensity of the fight—your vulnerability was intensity, and your survival strategy was leaving."[12]

I recognized that differing vulnerabilities were causing an unhealthy cycle in our relationship, and I didn't want it to continue. We were determined to squash whatever was going on beneath the surface of our disagreements, and that started with getting honest with each other. As time has gone on, we've uprooted different

119

"vulnerabilities," as Caroline Leaf puts it, broken down our past survival strategies, and determined where we want to go as a team.

REFLECTION QUESTIONS
• Do either of you routinely feel angry when certain conversation topics come up? • What steps are you going to take to experience healing from your hurt?

When You Feel Misunderstood

I love the story of the woman at the well in John 4. I have read it many times, but the Lord shook me during a recent read. If you're unfamiliar with the story, Jesus was venturing through Samaria with his disciples and stopped at a well for some water. He asked a Samaritan woman for a drink of the water that she had collected, and she was taken back by his willingness to talk to her and ask for a drink. Jews and Samaritans did not associate with one another. Jesus had stopped at this well during the hottest part of the day. Most women had gone to get their water at the beginning of the day to avoid the heat. However, this woman he met had not, and he knew there was a reason for that.

Jesus told her kindly,

"If you knew the gift of God, and who it is that is saying to you, 'Give me a drink,' you would have asked him, and he would have given you living water." The woman said to him, "Sir, you have nothing to draw water with, and the well is deep. Where do you get that living water? Are you greater than our father Jacob? He gave us the well and drank from it himself, as did his sons and his livestock." Jesus said to her, "Everyone who drinks of this water will be thirsty again, but whoever drinks of the water that I will give him will never be thirsty again. The water that I will give him will become in him a spring of water welling up to eternal life." The woman said to him, "Sir, give me this water, so that I will not be thirsty or have to come here to draw water." (John 4:10–15 ESV)

This woman was most likely shocked that a man was talking to her, and not just any man but a Jew! She was ashamed of her life, most likely, as she had a past with men that brought shame to her. Jesus, probably exhausted from his travels, met her here in the heat of the day and proposed something she had never heard about. He shared with her the cure to her thirst that she didn't know could be eternally cured.

Jesus went on to say she'd had five husbands and the man she was with then was not her husband. Jesus understood this woman more than anyone else cared to. On the surface, her own people judged her for not being able to keep a husband. In that day, a woman's worth was heavily tied to her husband. I can imagine she felt abandoned after five failed relationships. I wonder if she was just waiting for the next guy to leave her as well.

When Jesus entered the picture, she knew the minute he recalled her history that he was a prophet. He explained to her that he was the Messiah, and she went running back to the village to tell everyone she knew about the one who gave her living water. I bet for once in her life she finally felt understood, and not just understood by a stranger—but by *God*!

Not everyone, not even your future spouse, will understand you deeply in the way that Christ does. As much as some of our needs can be provided by our partner, only Christ can fill the deepest voids of our souls. When I feel misunderstood by my husband, it helps to know that I have access to God through my relationship with Jesus and he will fully provide for my every need when I ask him.

In Grief

Grief and fear of grief can control us in lots of different ways. I've noticed that Nick is slowly getting rid of the fear of his parents' deaths, but we've had many conversations that leave him with anxiety as he's walked himself through the inevitable happening one day. I've watched him lose a close friend before, and he handled it well, but a death in your own family can hit differently.

REFLECTION QUESTIONS

- What has grief looked like in your life?
- Have you ever lost a close friend when the two of you went separate ways? How did you handle that?
- Do you have any fears surrounding death or loss?

In Hurt and Disappointment

I used to seclude myself whenever something was hurtful to me or hard to talk about. I grew up seeing people close to me do the same thing to "escape" pain. What I didn't realize in these moments was that I wasn't escaping it—I was putting it off and eventually would have to deal with the hurt.

I can recall doing this and having it harm a friendship I had in my early twenties. The whole world was under a lot of stress with the pandemic in 2020, and I'm sure countless relationships were affected by that stress as people worked through personal issues. I had gotten into a disagreement with a friend, and out of fear that she would be upset with my opinion, I chose to ignore her, hoping the problem would go away and she would move on. Not surprisingly, my unhealthy approach to the situation led to miscommunication and wrong assumptions, and we eventually had to have a conversation to clear the air. If I would have just been honest from the start, the damage to our friendship could have been prevented.

REFLECTION QUESTIONS

- How have conversations gone in the past when you were upset with each other?
- Do either of you have disappointments that you are afraid might affect your relationship?

Emotional Abuse and Manipulation

I had a boyfriend in high school who used the fact that I was incredibly gullible to feed me lies to get what he wanted. I didn't realize it at the time, but I was being emotionally manipulated and, in the end, I was very hurt. He told me he had a relationship with God and even came to church with me. But later he admitted he didn't really have a spiritual relationship with the Lord and wasn't even sure there is a God; he only came to church to tempt me sexually. It's fine to have different beliefs, of course, but it is manipulative to lie about those things. Unfortunately, I allowed myself to be in situations with him where we were all alone, and I felt pressured to do what he said because he was domineering and had very little respect for my boundaries. It became clear that what I valued wasn't what *we* valued as a couple.

He mentioned to me once, after I got frustrated with him for pressuring me to do things I was not comfortable with, that he didn't understand why I had boundaries at all. If I loved him, why wouldn't I want to give all of myself to him? Those were the kinds of things he said to get me to feel shame about the boundaries that were meant to protect me. I thought I loved him at the time, but really I was in a bubble of manipulation, believing it was love. I hope you are never in a position like this. If you notice similar patterns in your relationship, hear my heart in this: you are better off single. Choosing to be with a person like this makes you start to believe that your next relationship will be no different. But the truth is, even if your past includes relationships like these, your future doesn't have to!

Red Flags of an Emotionally Unhealthy Relationship

- Avoids conflict and confrontation
- Acts more critical than supportive
- Behaves stubbornly and selfishly
- Acts defensive
- Creates more conflict than connection
- Always speaks negatively
- Has a negative outlook more often than a positive one

Attitudes and Actions You Want to See Instead

- Affirms your character
- Listens intently
- Shows respect for your boundaries and adopts them as their own
- Wants to process emotions with you (willing to grow)

I didn't realize before I got married how many moments I would have with my husband when we'd break down the emotions I never understood from my childhood as well as the issues I'm currently wrestling through as an adult. I never expect him to be my counselor, but in many ways, he helps me process like a counselor would. I understand every relationship is different, but having someone willing to walk through these moments with you is beautiful.

What If the Past Affects the Future?

One night in our marriage, Nick and I were lying in bed talking about how we felt distant from one another. Nick said he felt as if I was treating him like a child, and in many ways I was. He had confessed a sin to me a few days before, and I had told him I forgave him. I believe I meant that, but for the next few days I was hyperfocused on how he was doing and what he was doing. I wanted to keep tabs on him because I was fearful that what he confessed to me would happen again. I wanted to control the situation even though he had proven over time that this one recent mess-up was very unlike him. I was viewing him through the lens of fear. After our chat that night, I realized that I said I forgave him but ended up harboring bitterness in my heart.

As we talked through why my response was to become angry and resentful, I brought up the examples of men I had seen in my past. My parents are incredible, but I grew up seeing husbands cheat on their wives in the marriages of my friends' parents. From seeing that happen, I had developed a fear in my heart that my husband might cheat on me one day. I didn't realize it was there until we talked through it and prayed over what was going on in my heart . . . and I released that fear to God. Nick reassured me that he is committed to me and only has eyes for me.

I wonder how many of us in relationships have fears in our hearts because of emotional trauma growing up. I don't know your upbringing, but I'm sure you've walked through some challenging times. You may have done some major healing and have no need for this process. If so, praise God! But for those who need a bit of help . . .

REFLECTION QUESTIONS

- Are you harboring bitterness at all right now?
- Have you projected any fears from your past onto your significant other?
- Do either of you need to forgive right now?

God has given us so much grace to learn and grow as we go through life. The same is true within your relationship. Expect growth and be willing to change if you notice a red flag within yourself or your relationship. But also give grace to one another because Christ has lavished his grace and mercy on you.

A Few Words from Nick

How you respond or react is both a major determining factor and a gauge of the health and well-being of any relationship or friendship. We know this now because we weren't so careful with our responses when we first started dating, or even in the early days of our marriage. Soon, though, we realized that our purpose was not to prove ourselves right to our spouse, as though they were our enemy, but to attack the issue we were dealing with together. I definitely regret certain moments when I got a little too heated and said something I didn't mean, or when I had to have the last word to win the argument. I never won. I never got any gratification from being arrogant and rude. In fact, I was the loser in those situations.

Maybe there have been moments like this in your life or relationship too. One important thing to take to heart is that just because you've been going about things the same way some time doesn't mean you can't change your approach in the future. In fact, those who aren't learning new things and evolving tend to be the most unhappy people. Emotional intelligence starts with self-awareness, and self-awareness is something you can learn. You and your partner must be aware of how you are feeling, what is causing those feelings, and how you can communicate them in a way that is not demeaning but seeks resolution. When I'm upset, I'll often think for a moment and say something like this to Chelsea: "For some reason I'm feeling a bit of anger right now over what you said a minute ago, and I'm trying to sort out why that is. I'm not mad at you, but I am mad. Can you help me figure this out?"

It is imperative to remember that our partner is not our enemy. We do not attack one another. We do not attack the other person's point of view. We attack problems and issues that arise, and we do it together.

#10 ARE YOU SPIRITUALLY MATCHED?

Nick

I became a Christian when I was fourteen years old. I knew that I was broken, lost, and hurting, and I knew when I heard the gospel that it was far too good of an offer to pass up! However, I noticed that a battle continued under the surface even though I had become a believer. You see, just because I was now a Christian didn't mean that I wasn't tempted in every way, especially pertaining to lust.

In our chapter on purity, I shared how I began dating a girl when I was seventeen. We had every intention of honoring God and each other, but eventually we both gave in to sexual temptation. It became clear that neither one of us was mature enough to handle a romantic relationship, and even further, we were not spiritually matched as Christians. The Bible calls this "equally yoked." This was something I'd heard about, but I thought if the person I was dating claimed to be a Christian, then I was good to go! I quickly found out that I really should've done what God had called me to do and chose someone who wanted to live in Christ as tenaciously as I wanted to.

When it comes to your relationship, don't settle for someone who wears the title of "Christian" but doesn't truly live the life of a Christian believer. You don't have to look far to find a guy or girl who claims to be a Christian because growing up they went to church on Christmas Eve, or because their grandfather was a Sunday school teacher ten years ago. A Christian is not a title you wear; it is a life you live fully surrendered to Jesus and his ways. If Jesus is truly the Lord of our lives, then he is the one who gets the final say. We get to (not have to) delight in following him and his plans for our lives. I made a tremendous mistake in this area and didn't listen to what God asked of me, and as a result I went through an arduous season of grief, guilt, and feeling like I had failed God. I knew that I hadn't failed him, as he continually reminds me, but it was tempting to believe that I had.

We often believe that if we date someone who doesn't passionately follow Christ like we do, we can somehow convince them to change their ways. This is called "missionary dating," and I'd advise you to run far and fast from this way of thinking. Here is why: what happens more often than not is that when a passionate believer and a lukewarm believer date, the lukewarm believer distracts the passionate believer from following Christ. It is almost never the other way around. Do your best to avoid missionary dating—I'll explain this further from a biblical angle later in the chapter.

What I Learned

I realize I've mostly been speaking to the person who is already a passionate Christ follower—but if you are reading this and you find yourself uncertain, or maybe you have no real spiritual beliefs at all, then I want to encourage you to seek Jesus with your whole heart. Open yourself up to him, and begin reading the Bible. However, if you've determined that you do not believe the Bible and Jesus, or you just simply don't desire to live a passionate faith life, then I would still advise you: make sure you're not paired up with someone who has differing views on these matters. This level of disconnect will affect everything in your relationship, from your views on marriage and divorce, morality, childrearing, politics, and more. Differences in views here can and will cause a rift in the relationship.

It doesn't matter your background, past, or beliefs. I'm simply asserting that when two people of two different inward convictions seek to match themselves in marriage, that relationship usually struggles. And if we truly love someone, we don't want to force them to adjust and adapt their convictions for our sake. You're so much better off letting them go, for their sake and yours.

Have you ever heard the saying that a chain is only as strong as its weakest link? While we dare not evaluate someone's worth based on their "strength" or walk with Christ, we can make some assessments about their growth and maturity (or lack thereof) in their Christian walk. I don't think it is far-fetched to assume that a relationship is only as strong as its spiritual makeup and maturity.

What Being Equal and Unequal Looks Like

Here are a few things to look at in your relationship to see if you are a good spiritual match as Christians.

If a couple is unequally yoked on a spiritual level, there will usually be some clear signs, like one person wanting to go further sexually than the other; the Christian loosening up on their convictions to appease their partner; or a lack of agreement on ethical issues, politics, and an overall worldview. One of the most telling signs is the inability to have meaningful discussions about things of a spiritual nature. This might look like one person trying to contribute and provide meaningful detail and depth to the conversation but getting only shallow responses or requests to change the subject. If you find yourself in a relationship where you constantly worry or stress about having disagreements over important topics, then something deeper could be going on.

You can know for certain that you're in a relationship where a premium is placed on living vibrantly for Christ when you see a hunger in both of you to grow in your journeys with Jesus. You will find you can have meaningful conversations that display humility, empathy, and real interest in the other person's journey. You will find that you often pray for one another and you may potentially pray together as well. An equally yoked romantic relationship for Christ should involve agreement about church attendance and excitement about attending together if possible. This kind of relationship will develop a mutual understanding of personal holiness and a devotion to honoring God together. You'll pursue purity in the relationship and agree to wait to have sex until marriage.

What the Bible Says

The primary verse that points to this idea of being with someone of spiritual equivalence in the Christian union of marriage is from 2 Corinthians 6:14–16: "Do not be unequally yoked with unbelievers. For what partnership has righteousness with lawlessness? Or what fellowship has light with darkness? What accord has Christ with Belial? Or what portion does a believer share with an unbeliever? What agreement has the temple of God with idols? For we are the temple of the living God; as God said, 'I will make my dwelling among them and walk among them, and I will be their God, and they shall be my people'" (ESV).

Knowing the context here is helpful for gaining understanding of what this passage is teaching. "A yoke is a wooden bar that joins two oxen to each other and to the burden they pull. An 'unequally yoked' team has one stronger ox and one weaker, or one taller and one shorter. The weaker or shorter ox would walk more slowly than the taller, stronger one, causing the load to go around in circles. When oxen are unequally yoked, they cannot perform the task set before them. Instead of working together, they are at odds with one another."[13] In modern terms, when a strong and seasoned Christ follower begins a relationship with an unbeliever, problems navigating the relationship arise soon after. This has been the case numerous times in my life and in the lives of many friends and family members. I had to learn this concept the hard way, finding myself wandering in circles through relationships. Learn from my mistakes rather than re-creating them.

So what is Paul trying to get across in this passage? He is making the point that if we are joined to someone who has not agreed with us in the matters of our Christian life, we may very well sabotage the plans and purposes that God has for us. As we can see, Paul is using very colorful language to drive his point home, helping the Corinthians see that believers and unbelievers of Jesus can be friends, can sit over coffee and talk about how life is going, can sit around dinner tables and eat together, but they should not link lives in marriage. The mission and purposes of God take precedence over our own preferences and desires.

I want to go a bit deeper and discuss why I believe Paul feels so strongly about this. This passage was written to the church in Corinth, a church amid a very wicked city widely known for its sexual perversion, orgies, and the like. Paul noticed what was happening in this particular city and wrote to the church there urging them to flee these kinds of behaviors (1 Corinthians 6:18). Not only this, but as the church began to grow, there was a flurry of differing beliefs in the city. Whether it was pagan idolatry, Judaism, or something completely different, Paul began seeing strong Christian believers, both men and women he cared about deeply, falling away from their faith in Christ. Paul realized that who people—specifically Christians—were married to had a huge impact on their faithfulness to Christ.

I believe the best approach you can take to finding the right person is to figure out how you will honor and obey God and then to move in whatever direction he calls you, rather than looking high and low for "the one." Too many people decide to be unequally yoked because they're scared that God won't provide someone for them, so they settle for second best. Don't be that person. Have a bold and fearless resolve that God is who he says he is and that he will do what he has said he will do. His plan for you is always better than the second best you may be tempted to settle for.

What to Do Next

In the most ideal scenario, you are reading this as a man or woman of God who is either (1) single and looking for a relationship with someone else who loves God or (2) already in a relationship with that person. You are not perfect, but you are committed to a relationship centered on the supremacy of Christ and his Word, purity, transparency with others, maturity in every area, and an intention to marry this person so that you might bring more glory to God together than if you were separate.

If you find yourself having second thoughts on any front of your relationship, I suggest you find a trusted mentor or adviser and talk through the things that are bothering you. The worst thing you could do at this point is simply push past red flags and make them seem like no big deal. It is crucial that you do your due diligence here, and your partner should too. If you find yourself at odds with your partner, don't hesitate to take time to pray and ask God for his wisdom regarding your relationship. Most of all, be intentional to listen for the voice of God. Let the Word of God be the primary informer of your decision making and not anyone else.

REFLECTION QUESTIONS

Here are some questions I hope are helpful in this process.

- Are my partner and I currently honoring God in our relationship? What does that look like for each of us? Are we on the same page?
- Are we having meaningful discussions about what we believe God is doing in our lives and relationship?

- Do we see ourselves as equal in spiritual maturity? Why or why not? Do we see that changing?

  If you find that your answers reveal significant differences in your faith journeys, I recommend that you don't seek to "try harder" or "do better" so you can stay together and salvage the relationship, but that you consider loving one another enough to allow each other to grow in spiritual maturity outside the context of a relationship.

  Therefore let us leave the elementary doctrine of Christ and go on to maturity. (Hebrews 6:1 ESV)

A Few Words from Chelsea

For Nick and me, it took some time to figure out if we were ready to be in a relationship together. But as we prayed, the Lord made it clear that we were ready to take our relationship as friends to the next step. One of the most foundational aspects of our relationship was having older mentors speak into the major decisions we made together and individually. They warned us when they thought we might be making a poor decision, and they affirmed the growth they saw in us. They gave us resources, prayed for us, and encouraged transparency with each other. Pray for mentors in your life! Ask God to reveal a mature couple and ask them to mentor you. I promise it's not as scary or weird as it sounds.

SO WHAT NOW?

Nick and Chelsea

Can we just pause right here and acknowledge and celebrate you for a moment? You've dealt with a lot as you've gone through this book. You have read and pondered things that might have made others uncomfortable. You have wrestled with tension and have sought to gain a full understanding of your relationship. We are so excited for what is next in your personal life and your dating life.

Where do you go from here? It's easy to read a book like this and pick up some good insights and one-liners, but how do you actually put these things into practice and walk out what you've learned? More than anything, we hope and pray that this book has already caused you to have some important conversations with your partner—or that you will begin having those conversations in the future—to be sure one way or the other whether this is the right person for you. Not many other life decisions will have so great an impact on your future as this decision will, and of course you want to get it right.

While this process might have been uncomfortable in some areas, it was probably incredibly freeing in others. Maybe you were surprised about some of the things that came to light in the process of opening up, sharing, and talking through the issues covered in this book. These ten things we've presented as crucial to determining whether your partner is right for you are not just from our own experiences or worldly wisdom; we've found them all in the Bible, and they have stood the test of time. God has never let us down, and he won't let you down either. We encourage you to cling tightly to him as you deliberate whether this is the right relationship for you as you move closer to marriage.

Run with It (Nick)

Something you'll begin to notice rather quickly as you ramp up and lean into these conversations with one another is a lot of strong convictions. These strong convictions are a good thing, and I want you to lean into them as much as you can. They will help you as you move toward one of two places: a breakup or a future. Through these ten areas of discussion, you've determined that you and your partner are either not on the same wavelength when it comes to some pretty important topics, or you can see yourself having a future with your partner in a healthy marriage.

Hopefully these convictions and conversations will spark a sense of momentum in your life and in your commitment to honoring God, honoring each other, and allowing people to see Jesus in your relationship. If there is one thing I want to leave with you, I would encourage you to seek Jesus with even more intensity and tenacity than you ever have before. I've searched high and low and everywhere in between for the source of genuine, long-lasting joy. I never found it in a liquor bottle, at parties, with the in-crowd, in a flashy car or swanky house, in sex, or even in my marriage. Now, let me be clear: my marriage is wonderful, but it is not the source of my joy. That's an unfair burden to place on my spouse. My joy is in Jesus and in him alone. I believe yours can be too.

What Is God Saying? (Chelsea)

I can remember clearly a moment in my life when I chose not to listen to the Lord. I was a freshman in college at a school in California. The first week was amazing. I felt like I was creating a life that was exhilarating in comparison to the small-town life I lived in Illinois. I was dating my boyfriend (not Nick) long-distance, and we were determined to make it work. The second week I was there, I went to a church service and was worshiping with others. I heard the Lord say that I needed to break up with my boyfriend. That message shook me and I felt devastated. I didn't want to believe that was God speaking to me, so I tried to rationalize what I'd heard in my head, deciding it was just my own thoughts. But I continued to have a pit in my stomach. I couldn't shake what I heard and the fact that I was attempting to pretend as if life was fine. Not really sure what to do, I shared with my boyfriend what I believed the Lord was telling me to do. He didn't understand, so I made a deal with him (here I was, negotiating out of this relationship). I told him we should take a month to pray about either staying together or breaking up. He agreed with the plan, but I couldn't last a month. I flew home about two weeks into my college experience, dropped out of that school, started at a community college, and broke up with him. I knew there was a reason God wanted me to be single and out of that relationship, even if I couldn't have told you exactly why.

After some time and prayer, I realized that I'd had too much of my identity wrapped into that relationship and had been looking for my boyfriend to meet a need in me that only the Lord could meet. The Lord cares more about who you choose to do life with than you do. As we've ventured into the waters of what it could look like for you to say "I do" to your significant other, what is God saying? What has he taught you? Your story is going to be much different than ours, but when the Lord is directing your steps, you will be sure of your yes or your no!

Look for Progress, not Perfection (Chelsea)

I can recall a period of a few years when I was critical of every move my husband made. The way I went about "encouraging" him to grow was rude and snarky. As much as you may desire change at your pace, remember that your partner is on their own timetable with God. There is nothing you can do in your own power to force a change within your significant other. They have to want to change.

As our book comes to a close, there could be a temptation to forget all that could be put into practice. This journey is not always seamless, but choosing to walk the road of change for yourself is life changing! It is going to be easy to allow yourself to fall back into old ways and old patterns, but you have the Holy Spirit to help as you make incredibly important life decisions such as who you choose to spend your life with. This is your defining moment, a chance to draw a line in the sand as you move forward into your future. But even in the times you mess up or don't get it exactly right, I want to encourage you to look for the breakthrough in the messiness rather than beating yourself up for not getting absolutely perfect. If you search for nothing but perfection, you'll feel overwhelmed and have a hard time moving forward and seeing signs of progress. Focus on the wins and the small things you are getting right. The conversation that could've been an argument, but you chose to listen. The time you decided to stop kissing in the car after that date because you didn't want it to go too far. The time you thought about grabbing their phone to see who they were talking to, but you decided not to out of trust. Or that time they really annoyed you, but instead of lashing out, you shared your feelings calmly and graciously. The small wins matter, and I want you to celebrate them. It won't all come together in one instance, but it was never supposed to. Keep moving forward step by step.

Here are some benchmarks of growth that you can celebrate!

- Empathy in your relationship is growing.
- The result of disagreements is clear understanding.
- You feel confident in your decision to marry.
- You're not talking over each other in conversations (active listening).

• You've decided to go to counseling to work out past emotional trauma.

Ready for Marriage? (Nick)

I remember the first time I was asked this exact question. I remember the day, where I was, and who I was talking to. I could even take you to the exact table we were at in that little breakfast diner. When I think back to that day, I remember how I felt as well. I felt confident, and I assumed all the bases were covered since I was as ready as I could possibly be to get married. Then I got married, and of course there were things I didn't know. Things I hadn't thought about or considered. That's going to be your story too. There are things you just don't know until you experience them. Unfortunately, last I checked, that old saying still rings true: "You don't know what you don't know."

So, I present to you the very question I was asked those years ago. Take a deep breath. You'll be okay. But I want you to say these words aloud, because something tangible and real shifts in your thinking when you ask yourself this question out loud. You ready? Here it is: "Am I ready to get married?" You might already have your answer. Or you might still be unsure. Whatever the case, you're not wrong or right for any answer. Now, I want you to imagine that you are fifteen years older, sitting down with someone in your exact same shoes and in your exact same relationship right now. They have come to you in trust and confidence, asking you for your help as they decide whether they should marry the person they are with.

In light of the information, insight, and wisdom this book has sought to invest into your life, what would you advise them to do? Would you advise them to move forward toward marriage, or to think about breaking things off? By this point in the book, I'm guessing you have a pretty good idea as to which way the scales might be tipping in your particular case. I want you to trust yourself and trust that, based on everything you've seen thus far in your relationship, you can make the right choice.

The Big Payoff (Nick)

So what is the big payoff in all of this? I believe there is hardly anything better in this life than being sure of a decision you're making. Choosing whether or not to stay in a relationship is quite a big decision. Choosing who you will marry is an even bigger decision. It can feel like a lot of pressure if we allow it to, or we can lean into what the Holy Spirit is guiding us to do, what our gut is telling us to do, and what the facts are telling us to do. If these three are in agreement, I believe you have all the answer you need. If you still find yourself conflicted, I encourage you to take some time to pray and to seek the face of God and maybe the counsel of trusted advisers as well.

I love what King Solomon writes in Proverbs 3:5–6 (ESV): "Trust in the LORD with all your heart, and do not lean on your own understanding. In all your ways acknowledge him, and he will make straight your paths." Solomon, who is regarded as one of the wisest people ever to have lived, knew something that many of us need to be reminded of. We need to lean on God. While it's important to have assurance about a decision regarding a boyfriend or girlfriend, husband or wife, the biggest payoff of all is to have the opportunity to trust in Jesus wholeheartedly, choosing not to lean on ourselves and our own understanding to figure things out. I believe God is going to lay a straight path in the coming days as you trust and follow him.

One of the verses that has been especially meaningful to our family and to our marriage is Romans 15:13. Paul is writing to the church in Rome to help form their theology, as well as to inspire them with the hope we have in Jesus. As we come to the end of the road, at least for now, I want you to know that we have prayed this very verse over you; we have prayed that more than any advice, wisdom, or quick tips you find in this book, you will see the complete love of God over you and your unique situation, and that he will fill you with his hope, joy, and peace so that you might step into the fullness of his power at work in you.

> May the God of hope fill you with all joy and peace as you trust in him, so that you may overflow with hope by the power of the Holy Spirit. (Romans 15:13)

Ending in Prayer

Lord Jesus, thank you for forgiving me of my shortcomings and sins. You have so much patience and grace for me, and I am so thankful for that. Thank you for teaching me your character and your design for a healthy marriage. I give my future to you, and I ask that you would reveal areas in my heart where I have not surrendered control to you. I desire to have an emotionally healthy relationship, and to do so I need you to reveal areas of opportunity for my girlfriend/boyfriend to grow in as well. Form me into your image and help me where I fall short. If you want this relationship to continue, show me. If we're not the best fit for each other, provide a way out and help me walk in it confidently. Thank you, Jesus, for your mercy and healing. In your name I pray. Amen.

ACKNOWLEDGMENTS

Mom and Dad (Nick and Chelsea's parents)—we love you. Thank you for modeling what true love and commitment look like through thick and thin. Words will never express our gratitude and love for you.

To our Zondervan team (Webb, Carolyn, Devin, Sarah, Curt, Kim, Paul, Katie, Meaghan, and others)—we are so thankful for you believing in us and enabling us to bring this book to life.

To Trinity—thank you for assisting us in bringing this book to life from the very beginning.

To Clayton and Sharie—thank you for being a spiritual father and mother to us over the years. You've marked our lives in more ways than we can count.

To Hudson and Waldo, our golden retriever—thanks for being our writing buddies as we worked early mornings and late nights.

NOTES

1. Lorie Konish, "Couples Who Pool Their Money Are More Likely to Stay Together, Research Finds," CNBC, March 29, 2022, https://www.cnbc.com/2022/03/29/couples-who-pool-their-money-are-more-likely-to-stay-together.html.
2. Andrew Magers, "The Science of Sex before Marriage," *The Well Clinic* (blog), February 20, 2020, https://mywellclinic.com/blog/2020/02/20/science-sex-marriage/.
3. Joan R. Kahn and Kathryn A. London, "Premarital Sex and the Risk of Divorce," *Journal of Marriage and Family* 53, no. 4 (1991): 845.
4. Scott Stanley and Galena Rhoades, "Premarital Cohabitation Is Still Associated with Greater Odds of Divorce," Institute for Family Studies, October 17, 2018, https://ifstudies.org/blog/premarital-cohabitation-is-still-associated-with-greater-odds-of-divorce.
5. "Pornography Statistics," Covenant Eyes, accessed January 3, 2022, https://www.covenanteyes.com/pornstats/.
6. "Pornography Statistics."
7. Destin N. Stewart and Dawn M. Szymanski, "Young Adult Women's Reports of Their Male Romantic Partner's Pornography Use as a Correlate of Their Self-Esteem, Relationship Quality, and Sexual Satisfaction" *Sex Roles: A Journal of Research* 67 (May 6, 2012): 257–71, https://doi.org/10.1007/s11199-012-0164-0.
8. Jason S. Carroll et al., "The Porn Gap: Differences in Men's and Women's Pornography Patterns in Couple Relationships" *Journal of Couple and Relationship Therapy* 16, no. 2 (2017): 146–63, https://doi.org/10.1080/15332691.2016.1238796.
9. Amanda M. Maddox, Galena K. Rhoades, and Howard J. Markman, "Viewing Sexually-Explicit Materials Alone or Together: Associations with

Relationship Quality," *Archives of Sexual Behavior* 40, no. 2 (April 2011): 441–48, https://doi.org/10.1007/S10508-009-9585-4; Samuel L. Perry, "Pornography and Relationship Quality: Establishing the Dominant Pattern by Examining Pornography Use and 31 Measures of Relationship Quality in 30 National Surveys," *Archives of Sexual Behavior* 49, no. 4 (January 2, 2020): 1199–213, https://doi.org/10.1007/s10508-019-01616-7; Kyler Rasmussen, "A Historical and Empirical Review of Pornography and Romantic Relationships: Implications for Family Researchers," *Journal of Family Theory and Review* 8, no. 2 (June 1, 2016): 173–91, https://doi.org /10.1111/jftr.12141.

10. Tanya J. Peterson, "What Are Emotionally Healthy Relationships?," HealthyPlace, accessed February 28, 2022, https://www.healthyplace.com /self-help/self-help-information/what-are-emotionally-healthy-relationships.

11. Jeanne Segal et al., "Improving Emotional Intelligence (EQ)," HelpGuide, updated July 2021, https://www.helpguide.org/articles/mental-health /emotional-intelligence-eq.htm, italics added.

12. Caroline Leaf, "How to Stop Sabotaging Yourself and Relationships + How to Use Conflict to Deepen Relationships (with Human Connection Specialist Mark Groves)," Dr. Leaf, February 14, 2021, https://drleaf.com /blogs/news/how-to-stop-sabotaging-yourself-relationships-how-to-use -conflict-to-deepen-relationships-with-human-connection-specialist-mark -groves.

13. "What Does It Mean to Be Unequally Yoked?," GotQuestions.org, accessed February 27, 2022, https://www.gotquestions.org/unequally-yoked.html.

From the Publisher

GREAT BOOKS

ARE EVEN BETTER WHEN THEY'RE SHARED!

Help other readers find this one:

- Post a review at your favorite online bookseller

- Post a picture on a social media account and share why you enjoyed it

- Send a note to a friend who would also love it—or better yet, give them a copy

Thanks for reading!